At Issue

| Political Corruption

Eileen Lucas, Book Editor

Published in 2019 by Greenhaven Publishing, LLC
353 3rd Avenue, Suite 255, New York, NY 10010

Articles in Greenhaven Publishing anthologies are often edited for length to meet page
requirements. In addition, original titles of these works are changed to clearly present
the main thesis and to explicitly indicate the author's opinion. Every effort is made to
ensure that Greenhaven Publishing accurately reflects the original intent of the authors.
Every effort has been made to trace the owners of the copyrighted material.

Cover image: Carlos Yudica/Shutterstock.com

Library of Congress Cataloging-in-Publication Data

Names: Lucas, Eileen, editor.
Title: Political corruption / Eileen Lucas, book editor.
Description: First edition. | New York : Greenhaven Publishing, LLC, 2019. |
  Series: At Issue | Audience: Grades: 9 to 12. | Includes bibliographical
  references and index.
Identifiers: LCCN 2018025299| ISBN 9781534503809 (library bound) | ISBN
  9781534504479 (paperback)
Subjects: LCSH: Political corruption—United States—Juvenile literature.
Classification: LCC JK2249 .P63 2019 | DDC 364.1/3230973—dc23
LC record available at https://lccn.loc.gov/2018025299

Manufactured in the United States of America

Website: http://greenhavenpublishing.com

Contents

Introduction

P olitical corruption, defined by Transparency International as "the abuse of entrusted power for private gain,"[1] has existed since the beginning of civilization. It was certainly on the minds of America's Founding Fathers as they worked to create a government of, by, and for the people. Records from the debates surrounding the drafting of the US Constitution reveal deep-seated concerns regarding the abuse of power.

James Madison, one of the Constitution's primary authors, believed that a key function of government in a free society was its ability to provide balance between the various competing interests that exist and act in the larger public interest rather than the narrow interest of a particular faction. He distinguished true self-government from government "by corrupt influence," which substitutes "the motive of private interest in place of public duty; converting its pecuniary dispensations into bounties to favorites, or bribes to opponents." A corrupt government, Madison wrote, enlists "an army of interested partisans, whose tongues, whose pens, whose intrigues and whose active combinations, by supplying the terror of the sword, may support a real domination of the few, under an apparent liberty of the many."[2]

In more current times, author and professor Zephyr Teachout maintains that a dangerous shift has occurred in attitudes and practices relating to political corruption since the final decades of the twentieth century. In *Corruption in America*, Teachout asserts that the Supreme Court has thrown out many of the rules that had been in place to protect American government from the forces of corruption. This has led to "an overflow of private industry involvement in political elections and the rapid decline in the civic ethic in Congress and the state houses" as well as the 2010 Supreme Court decision commonly referred to as *Citizens United*, dealing with campaign spending by organizations.[3]

Between the writing of the Constitution and the fallout from the *Citizens United* decision, the debate about what constitutes political corruption and under what circumstances it is or it is not a crime has continued to rage. Although its definition appears simple, the manifestations of political corruption are not. As authors Ray Fisman and Miriam A. Golden state in their book *Corruption, What Everyone Needs to Know*, "Corruption appears in many distinct forms and displays many shades of gray."[4] Many obviously corrupt activities—such as embezzlement, vote buying, and theft of public resources—are also illegal. However, there are others that fall in a gray area, where they may not actually be illegal, but are still deemed by many to be corrupt.[5] For instance, one might ask: Was it corrupt for US Treasury Secretary Timothy Geithner to become president of a company he'd been charged with regulating just over a year after leaving office? Perhaps it was not illegal, but whether or not it was in the public's best interest may be another story.

A brief selection of some of the most noteworthy proven cases of political corruption in American history includes the following:

- The Yazoo land scandal of the early 1800s: Essentially, Georgia state legislators were paid by speculators to sell land at discounted prices. Even after the state of Georgia determined that the deal had been corrupt and cancelled it, these investors continued to sell the land at inflated prices.
- The Credit Mobilier scandal of 1867: Several high-ranking congressmen who were all close supporters of former General of the Union Army and soon-to-be President Ulysses S. Grant were given or allowed to cheaply purchase stock in the Credit Mobilier of America company, which was involved in the funding and construction of the Union Pacific Railroad. These congressmen turned that stock into a huge pot of gold and clearly used their public positions for private gain.
- Tammany Hall politics of the mid-to-late-1800s: Boss William Tweed—one of the most famous members of New York's Tammany Hall—and his cronies ran New York City in the Civil War era as their own private money factory. Tweed's

corruption was said to have earned him approximately $200 million, an almost unimaginable sum of money for the time.

- The Teapot Dome scandal of the 1920s: After the Department of the Interior was given control of naval oil reserve lands, Secretary of the Interior Albert B. Fall converted public lands into personal gain when he accepted bribes in exchange for rights to the Teapot Dome Reserve in Wyoming, which he granted to the Mammoth Oil company. Upon investigation, Fall was found to have received over $100,000 in bribes.
- Operation Greylord in Chicago in the 1970s and '80s: The Cook County Circuit Court system based in Chicago was believed to be so corrupt that two federal investigations were undertaken to expose it. As a result of the investigation, several judges were sent to jail including Judge Thomas J. Maloney. During the years he spent on the county court bench, Maloney "fixed" as many as six murder trials and took bribes of up to $100,000 from gangs to convict members of other gangs for murder.
- The Watergate scandal: One of the most prominent examples of political corruption in US history began with a break-in at the Democratic headquarters in the Watergate Hotel in Washington, DC, by five members of president Richard M. Nixon's re-election campaign. Although not initially involved, Nixon found out about the break-in and did everything he could to cover it up. He was ultimately forced to resign as a result.
- Abscam: In 1978, the FBI set up a phony company called Abdul Enterprises to arrange political favors for a nonexistent oil sheik. Five congressmen, a US senator, and other officials were convicted of profiting by doing favors in what became known as the Abscam operation. FBI videotapes captured the corruption and greed of those involved.
- Corruption charges against Washington lobbyist Jack Abramoff: At the height of his lobbying career, Abramoff

owned two restaurants near the Capitol, bought a fleet of casino boats, and leased four arena and stadium skyboxes. After Abramoff pled guilty to charges of corruption and tax offenses in 2006, ten officials were also convicted, including the former House Majority Leader Dick Armey.

As this list shows, despite their best efforts the Founding Fathers were not able to make the United States corruption-proof. Currently, questions regarding the possibility of illegal actions on the part of one or both of the main political parties during the presidential campaigns and election of 2016 abound.

To some extent, the examples listed above represent failed attempts at corruption simply because they were found out. After all, corruption is meant to go unnoticed. In recent decades, however, the ubiquitous nature of social media and hand-held technology as well as internet-hosted data collection and storage systems have helped make incidents of corruption more visible.

Does this mean corruption is more widespread? It's hard to say. It's equally difficult to know for certain if these investigative, technological, and research techniques translate to better ways to intervene, punish, and—even better—prevent political corruption. But is it possible to entirely prevent it?

Some commentators present a fairly bleak answer. "Voting rights were never so universal," writes one, "but contributions from our financial oligarchy carry more weight among US officials than mere ballots."[6] Instead of providing political and economic equality, our laws sometimes seem created to expand the distance between the super-rich and everyone else.

And yet there are others for whom the answer to this question is a qualified yes. "We are tentatively hopeful that demands for—and expectations of—honest government are rising in the world today," write Fisman and Golden. They add, however, that "for corruption to be tackled effectively, people who are opposed to it have to coordinate their efforts."

The viewpoints compiled in *At Issue: Political Corruption* focus primarily on past and present incidents of corruption in the United States, but with a glance at the international picture as well. They include the perspectives of academic researchers and political commentators. By and large, they conclude that corruption happens, it is a problem with serious consequences, and if we ignore it, it is at our—and our country's—peril.

Notes

1. Ray Fisman and Miriam A. Golden. *Corruption: What Everyone Needs to Know*. New York: Oxford University Press, 2017. p. 25.

2. "In the name of James Madison," by Rodger Hodge, Politico, February 16, 2011. https://www.politico.com/story/2011/02/in-the-name-of-james-madison-049561.

3. Zephyr Teachout. *Corruption in America: From Benjamin Franklin's Snuff Box to Citizens United*. Cambridge, MA: Harvard University Press, 2016, p. 10.

4. Fisman and Golden, p. 23.

5. Fisman and Golden, p. 27.

6 https://www.politico.com/story/2011/02/in-the-name-of-james-madison-049561.

1

Where in the World Is Corruption Most Prevalent?

Esteban Ortiz-Ospina and Max Roser

Max Roser is an economist at the University of Oxford and the founder of Our World in Data. His research focuses on poverty, health, and the distribution of incomes. Esteban Ortiz-Ospina is a senior researcher for Our World in Data and focuses on economic development, the public sector, education, and a wide range of related aspects.

Political corruption has been a part of human societies throughout history and around the world. Using Transparency International's Global Corruption Index and other data sources, this excerpted viewpoint focuses on perceptions of corruption and examples of corrupt behavior worldwide, including the correlation between the traffic violations of foreign diplomats and perceptions of corruption in their home countries. It discusses various forms of corruption and how they impact countries around the world.

Corruption is a phenomenon involving many different aspects, and it is therefore hard to give a precise and comprehensive definition. However, at the core of most definitions of corruption is the idea that a corrupt act implies the abuse of entrusted power for private gain. Classic examples include bribery, clientelism, and

embezzlement. Other, often more subtle and sometimes even legal examples of corruption include lobbying and patronage.

While long-run data on corruption is very limited, historical examples suggest that corruption has been a persistent feature of human societies over time and space. Two such examples are the sale of parliamentary seats in "rotten boroughs" in England before the Reform Act of 1832, and "machine politics" in the US at the turn of the 19th century (Aidt 2003).[1]

The unethical and often illegal nature of corruption makes measurement particularly complicated. Corruption data usually comes from either direct observation (e.g. law enforcement records and audit reports) or perception surveys (e.g. public opinion surveys, or expert assessments). In this entry we discuss data from both sources and discuss their underlying limitations.

As we show, although precise corruption measurement is difficult, there is a clear correlation between *perception* and *behavior*; so available corruption data does provide valuable information that, when interpreted carefully, can both tell us something important about our world as well as contribute to the development of effective policies.

For example, the data from perception surveys suggests that corruption correlates with human development, and a number of studies exploiting rich data from law enforcement records have shown that education is an important element explaining this relationship. Specifically, the data provides support for the idea that voters with more education tend to be more willing and able to monitor public employees and to take action when these employees violate the law.

Empirical View

Where Is Perceived Corruption Highest

The non-governmental organization Transparency International (TI) estimates a "Corruption Perception Index," which is arguably the most widely used indicator of corruption worldwide.

The Corruption Perception Index scores countries on a scale of 0-100, where 0 means that a country is perceived as highly corrupt and 100 means that a country is perceived as very clean. The indicator is representative of expert opinion, as it is constructed by taking the averages of various standardized expert surveys, including those from the Bertelsmann Foundation, the World Economic Forum, the World Bank, and many others.[2]

While TI's Corruption Perception Index has been estimated since 1995, the methodology has changed recurrently up until 2012. Because of this, the data discussed below starts in 2012.

The five countries with the highest scores (and thus perceived as most "clean") are Denmark, Finland, Sweden, New Zealand and the Netherlands. At the other extreme, the countries with the lowest scores (and highest perceived corruption) are South Sudan, Sudan, Afghanistan, North Korea and Somalia.

Over the time period 2012-2015, we can see that scores are fairly stable, and drastic changes in ranking are not very common. There are, however, some clear exceptions—Greece, for example, improved its score from 36 to 46 in the period 2012-2015 (which corresponds to a change in world ranking from 94 to 58).

Where Do People Perceive Corruption to Be a Major Problem?

The data relies on the perception of experts (e.g. business people, country analysts, etc.). Now we analyze data representing the perceptions of everyday people confronting corruption around the world.

The Global Corruption Barometer, also produced by Transparency International, surveys individuals around the world, asking them about their opinions and experiences regarding corruption.

Everyday people's perception of the problems associated with corruption correlates with expert opinion (seen in the previous section) about how much corruption there is. However, the correlation is far from perfect, indicating that these two indicators present us with different perspectives. An important example is

Sudan, which according to the Global Corruption Barometer has one of the lowest average ratings (meaning that average people do not consider corruption in the public sector to be a major problem). This stands in stark contrast to expert opinion, which regards Sudan as having among the highest levels of public sector corruption.

The fact that the perception of experts and other citizens diverge is at the heart of *perception* measures: experts and non-experts have different reference points against which they assess whether corruption is a problem. Indeed, in countries where the public finds corruption extremely intolerable, the perception of its implications may be extreme, even if baseline corruption levels are lower than in other countries.

Corruption is sometimes hard to tackle precisely because it is common, so people perceive it to be a natural economic transaction: it is easier to act corruptly if there are many other individuals who think it is fine to be corrupt. This is the rationale behind "big-push" policies that aim to shift norms and perceptions.

[...]

Where Are People More Likely to Pay Bribes to Access Public Services?

Bribery is one of the most common forms of corruption. The following data shows the share of people who report having paid a bribe to access public services in the 12 months prior to the survey. The data comes from the Global Corruption Barometer, produced by Transparency International, and the public services in question are: education, judiciary, medical and health, police, registry and permit services, utilities, tax revenue and/or customs, and land services.

Once again, cross-country heterogeneity stands out. In countries such as Kenya, Yemen, Liberia and Sierra Leone, more than two out of three survey respondents report having paid a bribe within the past year. In Denmark, Japan, Finland and Australia, only one in a hundred reports having paid a bribe in the same window of time.

While these results do show that in some countries bribe paying is very rare, we have to take into account that these estimates come from ordinary people interacting locally. Many countries where ordinary people do not frequently pay bribes have far-from-perfect international records when it comes to international private-sector bribery.

How Does Petty Corruption Affect the Income of the Poor?

For those without money and connections, paying even small bribes to access basic public services such as public health or police can have important consequences. In fact, petty corruption in the form of bribes often acts as a regressive tax, since the burden typically falls disproportionately on the poor.

[…]

Petty corruption seems to act as a regressive tax: poor households tend to pay a larger share of their income on bribes to access public services.

Where Are Firms More Likely to Be Asked for Bribes?

Bribes are also requested from, and paid by, firms in the private sector. For a selection of countries, the percentage of firms experiencing at least one bribe payment request during 6 transactions dealing with utilities access, permits, licenses, and taxes. The data comes from the World Bank's Enterprise Surveys (2007-2013).

According to this source, close to 70% of firms report having been asked for bribes in Syria and Liberia. Whereas in countries such as Bhutan, Slovenia, Israel, Eritrea and Estonia, the corresponding figure is below 1%.

Which Countries Are Perceived by Business Executives as More Likely to "Export Corruption?"

In its most recent edition (2011), the Bribe Payers Survey asked 3,016 senior business executives in 30 countries around the world for their perceptions of the likelihood of companies, from countries

they have business dealings with, to engage in bribery when doing business in the executive's own country.

Based on the answers from the Bribe Payers Survey, Transparency International estimates the average of the scores given by all the respondents who rated each country (on a scale from 0 to 10, where 0 means firms always pay bribes in that country, and 10 means they never do). This gives the so-called "Bribe Payers Index."

Companies from China and Russia are viewed as the most likely to pay bribes. From a global perspective this is important, since China and Russia are becoming increasingly powerful players in international trade.

Transparency International also publishes its index results by sector. According to these estimates, "public works contracts and construction" is the sector where firms from industrialized countries are more likely to engage in international bribery.

Many Firms from High-Income Countries Engage in Bribery Across the World

The Foreign Corrupt Practices Act (FCPA) in the US was passed in 1977 with the aim of making the bribery of foreign officials illegal. [...]

These official records show that US firms have paid bribes in 80 countries since 1977—including in many OECD countries.

Diplomats from Countries with High Corruption Perception Tend to Break Traffic Rules Abroad More Often

Corruption is commonly defined as "the abuse of entrusted power for private gain." Here we provide evidence of how diplomats in New York City abused their diplomatic status to break traffic rules by parking illegally.

UN mission personnel and their families benefit from diplomatic immunity. In New York City, until November 2002, diplomatic immunity implied that UN mission personnel could park illegally and avoid paying the corresponding

fines. The data tracks average unpaid annual New York City parking violations per diplomat by the diplomat's country of origin, over the period November 1997-November 2002. The data comes from Fisman and Miguel (2007)[3], who in turn obtained information compiled by the New York City Department of Finance.

This "revealed-preference" measure of corruption among diplomats correlates positively with the survey-based measures of corruption we have already discussed. Diplomats from countries where corruption perception is low (e.g. Denmark) seem to be generally less likely to break parking rules abroad, even in situations in which there are no legal consequences.

While the correlation is obviously not perfect (e.g. Colombia has a high corruption perception but zero unpaid parking violations in the data) Fisman and Miguel (2007) show that, statistically speaking, the positive correlation between corrupt behavior by diplomats "abroad," and corruption perception "at home," remains after controlling for factors such as national income in the diplomats' home country or the diplomats' salaries. This evidence suggests that cultural norms are one of the factors that affect corrupt behavior.

OECD Countries Are Increasingly Providing Procedures for Public Officials to Report Corruption

Corruption is not something that only affects low income countries—and in fact, many high income countries have become increasingly aware of this in recent years.

[...]

Since 2000 many OECD countries have developed formal mechanisms to allow public officials to expose corruption ("whistle-blowing") more easily. Specifically, the data shows that the share of OECD countries that reported having legal whistle-blowing procedures went up from 44.8% in the year 2000 (13 out of 29 countries in the sample) to 79.3% in 2009 (23 out of 29 countries in the sample). Today, many of these countries supplement legal

provisions with internal rules (e.g. minimum requirements for whistle-blowing programmes).

In 1999, the OECD Convention on Combating Bribery of Foreign Public Officials in International Business Transactions was enacted. This convention established legal standards to criminalize bribery of foreign public officials in international business transactions. In 2009 this convention was revised with new measures. The CESifo research centre provides an overview of when different OECD countries signed this and other related conventions, such as the UN Convention Against Corruption. As this evidence shows, legal provisions to fight corruption are something rather new, and high income countries are still trying to find new policy instruments to deal with corruption.

Correlates, Determinants, and Consequences

What Is the Relationship Between Development and Corruption?

[...]

There is again a strong positive relationship: countries where people are more educated tend to have better scores in the Corruption Perception Index.

The relationship in the visualization above is just a correlation: there are many factors that simultaneously drive corruption and development. Education is an important case in point.

As we can see, there is again a strong positive relationship: countries where people are more educated tend to have better scores in the Corruption Perception Index.

A number of academic studies have tried to establish the extent to which this relationship is causal. Glaeser and Saks (2006)[4], for example, show that within the US, states that are better educated tend to be less corrupt—importantly, they show that this relationship holds even when using historical factors like Congregationalism in 1890 as a proxy for the current levels of schooling. In other words, they find that historical levels of education predict differences in levels of corruption across States

several generations later. This is consistent with other studies that support the theory that voters with more education tend to be more willing and able to monitor public employees and to take action when these employees violate the law.

What Is the Relationship Between Corruption and Accountability

One of the most widely accepted mechanisms of controling corruption is to ensure that those entrusted with power are held responsible for reporting their activities. This is the idea behind so-called "accountability" measures against corruption.[5]

People are less likely to pay bribes in countries where there are stronger institutions to support accountability.

In a recent paper, Ferraz and Finan (2011)[6] show that there is evidence that this relationship is causal. Specifically, they show that electoral accountability causally affects the corruption practices of incumbent politicians in Brazil. In municipalities where mayors can run for reelection there is significantly less corruption, and the positive effect of accountability via reelection is more pronounced among municipalities with less access to information and where the likelihood of judicial punishment is lower.

How Effective Are Top-Down Audits to Reduce Corruption?

A common policy prescription to fight corruption is to increase monitoring and punishments. The logic supporting such policies is straightforward: better monitoring and harsher punishments increase the expected cost of acting corruptly, so people rationally choose not to break the rules.

To test the extent to which monitoring and punishments effectively reduce corruption, economists often rely on "policy experiments," where they administer these policies to "treatment groups." Olken (2007) follows this approach, increasing the probability of central government audits from 4 percent to 100 percent (the "policy treatment"), in the context of Indonesian village road projects.

Olken (2007) compares the outcomes for villages that received this intervention with those that did not and finds that audits

significantly reduced missing expenditures, as measured by discrepancies between official project costs and an independent engineers' estimates.

As we can see, missing expenditures were much lower in villages where audits were certain.

Olken (2007) provides further evidence of the extent to which officials in charge of road projects responded to private incentives: he finds that (i) audits were most effective when officials faced elections soon, and (ii) village elites shifted to nepotism (the practice of hiring family members), which is a form of corruption that was harder for audits to detect.

How Important Is the Link Between Cultural Norms and Corruption?

A recent study by Fisman and Miguel (2007)[7] shows that diplomats from countries where corruption perception is low (e.g. Denmark) seem to be generally less likely to break parking rules abroad, even in situations in which there are no legal consequences.

[…]

Fisman and Miguel (2007) show that the positive correlation between corrupt behavior by diplomats "abroad," and corruption perception "at home," remains after controlling for factors such as national income in the diplomats' home country or the diplomats' salaries. This evidence suggests that cultural norms are one of the factors that affect corrupt behavior.

[…]

Notes

1. "Rotten boroughs" were constituencies that had a very small electorate and could thus be used by a wealthy patron to secure influence; at the turn of the 19th century in immigrant US cities, "machine politics" involved hierarchical political organizations that provided social services and jobs in exchange for votes.
   For more information, see: Aidt, T. S. (2003). Economic analysis of corruption: a survey. The Economic Journal, 113(491), F632-F652.

2. The list of sources that are considered (subject to availability for each country) are: African Development Bank - Governance Ratings, Bertelsmann Foundation - Sustainable Governance Indicators, Bertelsmann Foundation - Transformation Index, IMD World Competitiveness Yearbook, Political Risk Services - Country Risk Guide, World Bank - Country Performance and Institutional Assessment, World Economic

Forum - Executive Opinion Survey, World Justice Project - Rule of Law Index, Economist Intelligence Unit - Country Risk Assessment, Global Insight - Country Risk Ratings, Political and Economic Risk Consultancy - Asian Intelligence, Freedom House - Nations in Transit

3. Fisman, R., & Miguel, E. (2007). Corruption, norms, and legal enforcement: Evidence from diplomatic parking tickets. Journal of Political Economy, 115(6), 1020-1048.

4. Glaeser, E. L., & Saks, R. E. (2006). Corruption in America. Journal of Public Economics, 90(6), 1053-1072.

5. Transparency International defines accountability as "the concept that individuals, agencies and organisations (public, private and civil society) are held responsible for reporting their activities and executing their powers properly."

6. Ferraz, C., & Finan, F. (2011). Electoral accountability and corruption: Evidence from the audits of local governments. The American Economic Review, 101(4), 1274-1311.

7. Fisman, R., & Miguel, E. (2007). Corruption, norms, and legal enforcement: Evidence from diplomatic parking tickets. Journal of Political Economy, 115(6), 1020-1048.

2

The Founding Fathers Were Corruption Fighters

John Joseph Wallis

John Joseph Wallis is a professor of economics at the University of Maryland and a research associate for the National Bureau of Economic Research.

America's founders grappled with the problem of corruption as they'd seen it in the governments of England, France, and other European countries. Their concerns ranged from moral and ethical values to the features of legal systems and political institutions. As the author of this viewpoint asserts, the constitutional reforms instituted in American political systems help safeguard this country against systematic corruption, which occurs when politics corrupts economics. In its entirety, the work maintains that American history provides an important lesson for modern developing countries about how to eliminate systematic corruption.

Ever since Aristotle identified that the "true forms of government, therefore, are those in which the one, the few, or the many govern with a view to the common interests," political philosophers and practitioners have been concerned about corrupt governments: those perverted forms that "rule with a view to the private interest" (1996, book III, 1279a, pp. 29–33). Aristotle, Polybius, Machiavelli and the sixteenth-century Italians,

"The Concept of Systematic Corruption in American History," by John Joseph Wallis, nber.org, March 2006. Reprinted by permission.

Harrington and the seventeenth- and eighteenth-century English writers who became known as Whigs or commonwealthmen, and Madison, Hamilton, and other American founders all grappled with the problem of corruption. Their search for an incorruptible form of true government required that they understand how corruption perverted government. Their ideas about corruption ranged from the moral and ethical values of princes and people to features of legal systems and political institutions. In the late seventeenth and early eighteenth century a specific concept of corruption, which I call "systematic corruption," crystallized in Britain and spread to the American colonies and France. Having identified the disease, all three societies spent a century or more designing and implementing constitutional reforms to protect their political systems against systematic corruption. Balanced or mixed government was the cure. Modern economic development was the result.

The reawakening of interest among economists about the role that political institutions play in determining economic performance has stimulated a renewed interest in the quality of governance and corruption. While corruption did not disappear from twentieth-century American politics, it has ceased to be a major concern. Concerns over corruption disappeared from American politics because Americans figured out how to control it. This suggests that a longer view of American history may offer insights into how economic and political institutions curb corruption.

The original idea behind this volume was to examine only the Progressive Era, but Americans began grappling with corruption long before the 1890s. As it turns out, Progressive Era reformers and twenty-first-century economists think about corruption in a way that is, in one critical dimension, 180 degrees removed from the concept of corruption that prevailed until the mid-nineteenth century. The title of McCormick's essay, "The Discovery that Business Corrupts Politics," captures the essence of the modern

concept of corruption, or, as Shleifer and Vishny define corruption, "the sale by government officials of government property for personal gain" (1993, p. 599).

In contrast, eighteenth-century British—English, Scotch, Irish, and American—political thinkers worried much more that the king and his ministers were manipulating grants of economic privileges to secure political support for a corrupt and unconstitutional usurpation of government powers. The commonwealth indictment of corruption in British government accused the Executive of subordinating parliamentary independence by granting economic privilege in a way that eroded balanced government and, with it, checks on the crown.

Commonwealth thinking shaped American colonial political thought and prepared the colonists to interpret the actions of Crown and Parliament after 1763 as unconstitutional threats to their fundamental liberties as British citizens. Once independent, Americans worried continuously about their governments and how to design their political institutions to limit corruption.

What I define as systematic corruption is both a concrete form of political behavior and an idea. In polities plagued with systematic corruption, a group of politicians deliberately create rents by limiting entry into valuable economic activities, through grants of monopoly, restrictive corporate charters, tariffs, quotas, regulations, and the like. These rents bind the interests of the recipients to the politicians who create them. The purpose is to build a coalition that can dominate the government. Manipulating the economy for political ends is systematic corruption. Systematic corruption occurs when politics corrupts economics.

In contrast, venal corruption denotes the pursuit of private economic interests through the political process. Venal corruption occurs when economics corrupts politics. Classical thinkers worried about venal corruption, too. They talked at great length about the moral and ethical corruption of entire peoples and

societies, as well as governments. They realized, however, that venal corruption is an inevitable result of human nature. So they focused their intellectual enterprise on designing and then protecting a form of government that could resist systematic corruption. By eliminating systematic corruption, they hoped to mitigate the problems of venal corruption as well.

[...]

The paper's fundamental conclusion is that the most basic economic institution in a modern, thriving, developed economy—unlimited free entry and competition unrestricted by government—developed as a solution to systematic corruption: a solution to the political problem of preventing narrow political groups from obtaining uncontested control of governments. The real lesson developing countries can learn from American history is how the United States eliminated systematic corruption. Eliminating systematic corruption required an economic solution to a political problem. Between the 1790s and 1840s, the United States developed a constitutional structure of state governments that mandated free economic entry and competition. It took seventy years, but the round of American state constitutional changes in the 1840s are the heart of what eliminated systematic corruption. American governments were so successful at eliminating systematic corruption that we no longer understand what the term corruption meant in the 1800s, nor do we worry about systematic corruption in our current political system.

Corruption, Revolution, and Constitutions

[...]

We have reached the point where British and American paths divide. The "republican synthesis" in American history provides a convincing explanation for why Americans revolted and what "made their revolution so unusual, for they revolted not against the English constitution but on behalf of it" (Wood 1969, p. 10). The desire to preserve the existing constitution made the American revolution one motivated by fear rather than hope. The widespread

perception of English corruption, on both sides of the Atlantic, inexorably drove the Americans to independence once a wedge opened between Parliament and the colonies in 1763. The fear in the American colonies was that England, "once the land of liberty—the school of patriots—the nurse of heroes, has become the land of slavery—the school of parricides and the nurse of tyrants." At its root, the fear driving the American Revolution was Polybian. The influence of the executive in Parliament had unbalanced the constitution. What inevitably followed monarchy, no matter how pure the intentions of those who produced the monarchy, was tyranny. As Patrick Henry declared: "Our chains are forged. Their clanking may be heard on the plains of Boston!"

Any government organized along commonwealth lines should immediately have put in place a constitution with balanced government. In May of 1776, the Continental Congress asked the states to write their own constitutions. By July 3, New Jersey had drafted a new constitution which, among its many features, distinctly articulated the separation of powers:

> *XX. That the legislative department of this government may, as much as possible, be, preserved from all suspicion of corruption, none of the Judges of the Supreme or other Courts, Sheriffs, or any other person or persons possessed of any post of profit under the government, other than Justices of the Peace, shall be entitled to a seat in the Assembly: but that, on his being elected, and taking his seat, his office or post shall be considered as vacant.*

The Constitution of Maryland, ratified in November 1776, stipulated in Section 6 of the Declaration of Rights: "That the legislative, executive and judicial powers of government, ought to be forever separate and distinct from each other." Separation of powers was the most visible way that Americans addressed systematic political corruption, but the entire structure of early state constitutions, with their articulated branches, attempted to systematize balanced government. The powers assumed by the

states in their constitutions were not powers necessarily denied to the national government. But once states defined their powers they could not be taken by the national government without substantial political cost. The second national constitution, written in 1787, gave the national government broad and generous powers. But only in the areas of military and international affairs, public lands, international trade and commercial policy, and (to a lesser and immediately disputed extent) financial and monetary policy did the national government possess well-defined exclusive powers. Even in these areas, with the exception of military defense and international relations, the national government subsequently found it extremely difficult for political reasons to exercise its constitutional powers. National government action inevitably raised the specter of systematic corruption.

The ability of states to legislate, regulate, or promote almost any aspect of economic and social behavior meant that the states, and not the national government, became the focal point of economic policies. Americans were embarking on two new experiments in government: written constitutions and widespread government support of private organizations. The first experiment is a central part of American history. The second experiment, successful as it was, is so taken for granted that we rarely recognize how important government support of private organizations was for American social and economic development. As de Tocqueville famously noted: "Americans of all ages, all stations in life, and all types of dispositions are forever forming associations. There are not only commercial and industrial associations in which all take part, but others of a thousand different types—religious, moral, serious, futile, very general and very limited, immensely large and very minutes. . . . In every case, at the head of any new undertaking, where in France you would find the government or in England some territorial magnate, in the United States you are sure to find an association" (1966, p. 513).

The American colonists brought the ancient English constitution with them, but not a king or an aristocracy, two of the critical elements in the constitutional balance. This led to a more egalitarian society, a deep belief in the right of individuals to assemble, and more vigorous private sector organizations. In Europe, the right to form voluntary organizations was not universal; one found governments and territorial magnates at the head of organizations because they possessed the sometimes implicit, but often explicit, privilege to form organizations. The ability to form corporations was limited to the social and economic elite. Limited entry created the economic rents that made royal grants of privilege to the monied interests so valuable.

America's balanced state constitutions recognized the Harringtonian imperative of balancing power within the government in the same proportion as land ownership was balanced in the population. "Power results from the real property of society." The equality of land ownership posed new and vexing problems for American politicians, problems without English antecedents. The distribution of land did not mirror the distribution of social prestige or the presumed distribution of leadership talents within the "natural elite." Freedom of assembly, freedom of speech, and freedom of petition were fundamental rights. How far did these rights extend into the politically competent, independent, landowning citizenry? Who had the right to vote, to incorporate a business, or form a political party? Britain's financial revolution did not represent a move toward an economy or society with more open entry; it restricted entry. Adam Smith and the classical economists built their criticism of government policy on mercantilist limitations on access to economic organization. Kings and ministers used limited access to create economic rents, then used the spoils from the rents to purchase political influence, and thus eroded the independence of Parliament and corrupted the entire political system. Corporations and

stock-jobbers represented the very essence of both systematic and venal corruption. How was the United States to deal with the identical problem?

Corruption and the First Crisis of National Politics

Straightening out the nation's finances instigated the first battle over corruption in the new republic. Hamilton's proposed financial policies—refunding national and state debts, a national bank, a moderate revenue tariff, and excise taxes—all stimulated opposition and debate when Congress considered them in the first Congress, which ended in March of 1791. Each of Hamilton's measures raised fears of corruption in classic commonwealth terms, but all of them passed. The debate over the meaning of the new financial system in the summer of 1791, however, produced a conflagration of fears about systematic corruption and led to the creation of an opposition party in the United States. All of the policy measures at issue were economic, and the critical element in the debate was the effect of the economic policies on politics.

We have already seen how the financial revolution in England created a funded national debt, a bureaucracy of excise and tariff collectors, a national bank, and an interlocking set of financial intermediaries and chartered corporations that marketed and traded in government debt. As the bureaucracy expanded, so did opportunities for executive patronage. The ability to tie the interests of the financial community to the policies of the government through the medium of the national debt and corporate charters allowed the Crown to extend its influence and undermine the independence of Parliament. The danger of the English system of finance was to fundamental liberties; it was systematic corruption, and the identification of financial interests with the Crown was the mechanism of corruption.

Hamilton's arguments for America's new financial system had ominous overtones. In the Report on the Public Credit in January 1790, Hamilton proposed that "If all the public creditors receive

their dues from one source . . . their interests will be the same. And having the same interests, they will unite in support of the fiscal arrangements of the government."31 Hamilton proposed precisely the type of arrangement with the monied interest that commonwealthmen feared in Britain.

As Banning noted (1978), it would have been difficult to consciously design a financial program that provoked commonwealth fears of executive influence more directly than Hamilton's. The debate about the implications of the financial plan after it was passed in 1791 opened a division within the national government. On the Federalist side the Adamses, joined by Hamilton, praised the British constitution and argued against extending democracy too far. On what would become the Republican side, Jefferson and Madison, abetted by Thomas Paine and Phillip Freneau, attacked the Adamses as monarchists and Hamilton as an aspiring Prime Minister. The Republicans castigated the financial plan as an attempt by Hamilton to use his position as Treasury Secretary to secure control of the government through systematic corruption. Public acrimony between the participants set in motion the formation of distinct Federalist and Republican parties in national politics. The way in which the conflict was resolved placed corruption in governmental promotion of economic development at the center of American politics for the next seventy years. It took a long time for Americans to figure out how to write their constitutions. The conflict of the 1790s brought to prominence several contradictions in the American experiment with republican government.

Popular sovereignty versus tyranny of the majority. In the ratification debates, both the Federalists and the Anti-Federalists argued for popular sovereignty as a critical element in the new American system. Sovereignty, lodged with the people, could be delegated to representatives through election. Yet ultimately sovereignty remained in the hands of the voters. But to those steeped in commonwealth theory, tyranny of the many was just as much of a threat as tyranny of the one or the few. The exercise

of popular sovereignty necessarily involved the risk of tyranny of the majority, a risk that Madison and Hamilton both appreciated. Madison hoped the extended republic would mitigate the risk, as he argued famously in Federalist #10. The greatest danger from majority rule lay in the possibility that a demagogue would arise, unify a majority of the voters behind him, and lead the government into despotism. Such a leader might override the checks and balances built into system by sweeping a majority through all the branches of government. Madison's hopes didn't last a decade: by the early 1790s the Federalists controlled all three branches of the national government.

Political parties versus corruption. The Constitution itself offered a way for Jefferson and Madison to oppose the Federalists: the formation of an opposition party. The logic of the winner-take-all electoral process for President, as well as other offices, seemed to guarantee that two competing parties would eventually emerge.

[...]

Rather than stressing the need for competing parties, Madison and the Republicans emphasized the need for one government with the right policies. They claimed that they stood on the side of the angels in a debate over republican versus monarchical government and pure versus corrupt methods of governing. Tarring Adams and the Federalists with being closet monarchists played well to some voters, but it was the fear of executive influence in the legislature, wielded by Prime Minister Hamilton through the coordinating mechanism of the Bank of the United States and the national debt that posed the greatest threat. It was a threat that resonated with a century of British political writing and decades of American paranoia over corruption in the Britain. The negative political implications of the Republicans' existence as an organized political party were minimized by stressing the rightness of their cause. "The situation of the public good, in the hands of two parties nearly poised as to numbers, must be extremely perilous. Truth is a

thing, not of divisibility into conflicting parts, but of unity. Hence both sides cannot be right. Every patriot deprecates a disunion, which is only to be obviated by a national preference for one of these parties." If the Republicans were truly right, then their cause was not a partisan one but a righteous one, and when the country came to see the wisdom of their position there would no longer be a need for competing parties.

Corruption versus promotion of economic development. By building their case against Hamilton and the Federalists along traditional commonwealth lines, the Republicans gained the moral force of a century of British and American thinking about corruption in government. At the same time, they boxed themselves into a fundamental dilemma. The Republicans were just as pro-growth and development as the Federalists. Their arguments against the Federalists were political, not economic. They were not arguing that Hamilton's plan wouldn't work in economic terms, but that Hamilton was taking the first step down the slippery slope to executive tyranny. How then did the Republicans propose to promote economic development?

The only model available at the end of the eighteenth century was one that had been used by European governments to promote economic development for centuries: by creating public service corporations. Those corporations were given public privileges in order to induce them to provide public services. Their public privileges generated private rents by limiting entry. Drew McCoy's book, *Elusive Republic*, makes abundantly clear that the central tenets of Jefferson's and Madison's economic vision required the construction of a financial and transportation infrastructure to bring the agrarian west into viable production. At the same time, foreign economic policy had to ensure growing external markets for American products abroad, so that yeomen farmers did not produce themselves into poverty. There was no institutional vehicle to promote financial and transportation improvements but the corporation. If the Republicans condemned the corporation

as an instrument of corruption at the national level, they left themselves without a way of promoting the very economic development that they sought and that voters demanded. None of these contradictions were resolved in the first forty years of the country's history—all three were resolved in the 1830s and 1840s.

3

Modern-Day Politics and the Abuse of the Public's Trust

Voice of America

Voice of America *began broadcasting in 1942 to combat Nazi propaganda with accurate and unbiased news and information. Voice of America has worked to provide the world with truth, hope, and inspiration ever since.*

This viewpoint describes the Illinois governor's "pay-for-play" politics as a modern-day continuation of the so-called "machine"-style politics that were the norm in big cities like Chicago and New York from the mid-nineteenth century until the 1960s. The size and scope of the corruption the governor was accused of serve as a reminder that the temptation to use the public trust for private gain is still a force in American politics.

Americans were shocked this week by the boldness of the graft and other crimes allegedly committed by Illinois Gov. Rod Blagojevich, which included attempts to sell the vacated US Senate seat of President-elect Barack Obama to the highest bidder. But corruption is nothing new in American politics, although the scope and definitions of corruption have changed over time.

At a press conference in Chicago on Thursday, Obama reacted to the corruption charges against the Illinois governor by stating a stark truth about political power.

"Corruption in American Politics Has Long History," Voice of America, October 27, 2009. Reprinted by permission.

"I think in Illinois—as is true in American politics generally—there are two views of politics," Obama said. "There is a view of politics that says you go into this for sacrifice and public service, and there is a view of politics that says, 'This is a business.' And you're wheeling and dealing and 'What's in it for me?'"

Illinois politics is well known for a tendency toward the "what's in it for me" approach and the corruption that can breed. In 2006, the state's previous governor was sent to prison for six and a half years for fraud and other crimes, and according to *Slate Magazine*, 469 politicians from the federal district of northern Illinois were convicted on corruption charges between 1995 and 2004.

But Columbia University political science professor Justin Phillips says none of their crimes were as egregious as the ones of which Blagojevich has been accused.

"Corruption in American politics has typically been the trading of government contracts or government benefits for, oftentimes, just simply campaign contributions. You know, 'Here is some money into your campaign, and in exchange, you give me and my business a particular contract.' Or, 'I take you to a basketball game, give you some great seats, and in exchange, you give me something my client wants,'" Phillips says. "Those types of exchanges are typically what would we see when we talk about corruption in American politics."

If the exchange of goods and services for money is legitimate in the public marketplace, why is it considered immoral in politics? Kent Redfield, a political science professor at the University of Illinois and the author of several books on state politics and corruption, says politicians are elected or appointed to do the people's business, not their own.

"If they are benefiting personally from bribes, extortions and campaign finance contributions, then they essentially have a conflict of interest," Redfield says. "The question is: are they trying to pursue the public interest to do what's best in terms of their office ... or are they shaping policy in ways that guarantee they get the most money?

"So this distorts public policy. And if citizens ultimately believe that everything is for sale and it's corrupt, then they have no reason to support the political system."

Redfield describes Blagojevich's "pay-for-play" politics as a modern-day continuation of the so-called "machine"-style politics that were the norm in big cities like Chicago and New York from the mid-19th century until the 1960s. Machine politicians relied on new immigrants who had little political pull. In exchange for votes, party bosses would give the newcomers jobs once their candidates were put in office, or politicians would take bribes in exchange for ensuring the efficient delivery of city services, like snow or garbage removal, or the granting of lucrative city contracts.

"I guess, in a perverse way, that means if you've got enough resources, you can be ensured that things are going to get done unless somebody outbids you," Redfield says. "But, on the other hand, that's why those systems have problems [in the] long term. That only works for people who have resources, and that generates discontent. Those are the sorts of things that historically lead to political upheaval and revolutions."

On the other hand, says Phillips, political machines were quite effective at practical governance.

"They could get things done. Machines, because of their vast control and their ability to ... peddle influence, they got a lot done, where reformist governments in American cities were much less effective. And so the public in cities had a sort of love-hate relationship with the machines."

Ultimately, however, Phillips says legal reforms broke the power of the party machines.

"Number one, the requirements for registering to vote changed. So machines, as soon as immigrants got off the boat, they couldn't register them to vote and bring them into American politics.

"Other reforms made the quid pro quo [the exchange of favors] transactions that machines engaged in illegal. Increased efforts to change the government employment in this country to a civil

service system, as opposed to a system where everybody that worked in government was a political appointee.

"So the machine had fewer benefits to dole out. And as machines had fewer benefits, they sort of began to wither and die."

Under American legal principles, Blagojevich is presumed innocent until he is convicted of the crimes prosecutors have alleged. However, the size and scope of the corruption of which he has been accused are a reminder. Regardless of the legal sanctions Americans hope will ensure fairness in public life and selflessness in public officials, the temptation to use the public trust for private gain is still a force in American politics.

4

The Search for the Most Corrupt State in the US

Oguzhan Dincer and Michael Johnston

Oguzhan Dincer is an associate professor of economics at Illinois State University and a lab fellow at the Edmond J. Safra Center for Ethics. Michael Johnston is the Charles A. Dana Professor of Political Science at Colgate University and a lab fellow at the Edmond J. Safra Center for Ethics.

The authors of this viewpoint surveyed news and investigative reporters covering state politics and issues related to corruption during the first half of 2014 to create an index for measuring political corruption in American states. They differentiated between legal and illegal corruption. Illegal corruption is defined as the private gains in the form of cash or gifts by a government official in exchange for providing specific benefits to private individuals or groups, and legal corruption as the political gains in the form of campaign contributions or endorsements by a government official in exchange for providing specific benefits to private individuals or groups.

Although corruption is not endemic in America as it is in several other countries, it does exist. According to the Justice Department, in the last two decades more than 20,000 public officials and private individuals were convicted for crimes

"Measuring Illegal and Legal Corruption in American States: Some Results from the Corruption in America Survey," by Oguzhan Dincer and Michael Johnston, Charles A. Dana Professor of Political Science, Emeritus, The President and Fellows of Harvard College, December 1, 2014. Reprinted by permission.

related to corruption and more than 5,000 are awaiting trial, the overwhelming majority of cases having originated in state and local governments.[1] Understanding the causes and the consequences of corruption and designing the policies in the fight against it starts with measuring corruption itself. How do we measure corruption, an activity that requires secrecy? The most commonly used measure of corruption in American states comes from the Justice Department's "Report to Congress on the Activities and Operations of the Public Integrity Section." These data cover a broad range of crimes from election fraud to wire fraud. The measure, based on the Justice Department data, suffers from several significant problems, however.

1. The data report federal public corruption convictions; thus, corruption cases tried by state and local prosecutors are not included in the data. Federal prosecutors have considerable discretion over how much effort to put into investigating public corruption. Hence, the number of convictions depends not only on the level of corruption but also on levels of prosecutorial effort.[2] Prosecutors choose which cases to prosecute and which to decline so as to maximize their conviction rate and their visibility.[3]

2. The number of federal convictions is related to prosecutorial resources in a state.[4]

3. Partisan bias is likely in the prosecution of public officials by federal prosecutors, i.e., the US attorneys. The decision to prosecute is up to the US attorneys who are appointed by the President with the advice and support of the home state partisans. There is anecdotal as well as empirical evidence supporting this hypothesis. The unprecedented midterm dismissal of seven US attorneys in 2007, for example, led to congressional investigations. Some were allegedly dismissed either because they did not pursue corruption investigations against prominent Democrats with sufficient vigor or because they did pursue investigations against prominent Republicans.[5] Similar allegations have resurfaced in Virginia in 2014.

4. While data are reported annually, there is an unknown, and most likely variable, time lag between crimes and convictions.

5. The data give little to no indication as to the seriousness of a case.

6. The data cover only those officials who are caught and, of course, convicted.

There are other problems with measuring corruption by using conviction data, too. Over the three decades between 1980 and 2010, for example, South Dakota appears to be the most corrupt state—two and a half times more corrupt than New Jersey—as judged by federal convictions. This is quite surprising since the Dakotas were among the leading states in the movement against corruption in government that started in the late 19th century and continued through the 1930s.[6] Prairie states such as the Dakotas, Minnesota, and Wisconsin are historically the least corrupt in the US. In fact, the only perceptions-based index measuring state level corruption in the US ranked South Dakota as the least corrupt state in 1999.[7] Any index based on convictions standardized for population is likely to be more variable in states with small populations, like the Dakotas, because a handful of cases will affect rates much more there than in, say, New York or Texas. For example, the number of convictions per 1 million people in Louisiana increased from 7 to 14 between 1989 and 1990 and declined to 2.5 in 1991—doubling in one year and decreasing more than fivefold in the next. Other states show similar variability in convictions, even though it is unlikely that underlying levels of corruption are changing so markedly.

An alternative to a measure based on convictions is a measure based on perceptions. Several international organizations such as Transparency International have constructed indices to measure corruption across countries based on the perceptions of experts since the mid-1990s. The only attempt to construct a perceptions based index for American states was by Boylan and Long in the late 1990s. They surveyed reporters covering state politics in each

state and asked questions about public corruption. Unfortunately though, their survey was designed to construct an aggregate index covering all forms of corruption in all branches of government.

To be able to know where in state government to push for reform and to be able to measure the effectiveness of these reforms, we need to have a somewhat more disaggregated index measuring different forms of corruption in different branches of government. To construct such a disaggregated index, we surveyed the news reporters covering state politics in addition to the investigative reporters covering issues related to corruption during the first half of 2014. Boylan and Long make a compelling argument regarding why we should survey reporters rather than another group of professionals such as trial lawyers or small business owners to measure government corruption. Reporters have a better knowledge of state governments and spend a great deal of time observing the government officials and interacting with them. We identified close to 1,000 reporters through an extensive search of the internet and contacted them via email. Investigative Reporters and Editors, Inc. (IRE) helped us to contact the ones that we were not able identify on our own. We received a total of 280 responses. Unfortunately, in some states (Arkansas, Hawaii, Idaho, Massachusetts, Montana, North Dakota, New Hampshire, South Carolina, and South Dakota) only a small number of reporters responded to our survey. Hence while interpreting the results from these states we should be cautious. Surprisingly enough, we received no responses from Louisiana, which is historically one of the more corrupt states in America.[8]

Our main purpose is to construct perception-based indices measuring two specific forms of corruption across American states: illegal and legal. *We define illegal corruption as the private gains in the form of cash or gifts by a government official, in exchange for providing specific benefits to private individuals or groups.* It is the form of corruption that attracts a great deal of public attention. A second form of corruption, however, is becoming more and more

common in the US: legal corruption. *We define legal corruption as the political gains in the form of campaign contributions or endorsements by a government official, in exchange for providing specific benefits to private individuals or groups, be it by explicit or implicit understanding.* Such dealings are, in turn, one aspect of the broader issue of institutional corruption which, according to Lessig,

> *is manifest when there is a systemic and strategic influence which is legal, or even currently ethical, that undermines the institution's effectiveness by diverting it from its purpose or weakening its ability to achieve its purpose, including, to the extent relevant to its purpose, weakening either the public's trust in that institution or the institution's inherent trustworthiness.*[9]

According to several surveys, a large majority of Americans, both liberals and conservatives, think that donations to super PACs, for example, by corporations, unions, and individuals corrupt the government.[10]

We asked reporters how common were these two forms of corruption in the executive, legislative, and judicial branches of the government in 2013 in the state they cover in their reporting in 2013. The response scale ranged from "not at all common" to "extremely common." For each reporter responding to the survey, we assigned a score of 1 if he/she chose "not at all common," 2 if he/she chose "slightly common," and so on. The score of 5 meant that the reporter responding to the survey perceived corruption to be "extremely common."

Illegal Corruption in America

In none of the states is illegal corruption in government perceived to be "extremely common." It is nevertheless "moderately common" and/or "very common" in both the executive and legislative branches in a significant number of states, including the usual suspects such as California, Florida, Illinois, New Jersey and Texas. Arizona is perceived to be the most corrupt state with legislative

and executive branches both scoring 4. Among the states in which the legislative and executive branches are perceived to be corrupt, only in Florida and Indiana is illegal corruption in the judicial branch perceived to be "not at all common." Idaho, North and South Dakota and the majority of the New England states—Massachusetts, Maine, New Hampshire, and Vermont—are perceived to be the least corrupt states with all three government branches scoring 1.

Executive Branch

In more than ten states, executive branches score 3 or higher in illegal corruption. In no state is illegal corruption in the executive branch perceived to be "extremely common" by the reporters. It is, on the other hand, "very common" in Arizona and New Jersey, and somewhere between "moderately common" and "very common" in Georgia, Kentucky, and Utah.

Legislative Branch

State legislators are perceived to be more corrupt than the members of the executive branches in a number of states. In almost half of the states, legislative branches score 3 or higher in illegal corruption. In ten states, illegal corruption in state legislatures is perceived to be "very common." Among the states in which legislative branches score 4, New York and Rhode Island are particularly interesting since illegal corruption is perceived to be only "slightly common" in the executive branches in these two states.

Judicial Branch

No states score 3 or higher in illegal corruption in judiciary. Nevertheless, even a score of 2 is still worrying since it is the judicial branch of the government that is supposed to try and convict the corrupt officials. In California, for example, illegal corruption in the judiciary is perceived to be somewhere between "slightly common" and "moderately common." Both the executive and legislative branches in California are also perceived to be corrupt with the scores of 3 and 4, respectively.

Legal Corruption in America

Legal corruption is more common than illegal corruption in all branches of government. Executive and legislative branches score 3 or higher in legal corruption in a large majority of states. In seven states, legal corruption in the judicial branch is perceived to be "moderately common" and in Nevada it is perceived to be "very common." In ten states, both legislative and executive branches score 4 or higher and in Kentucky and New Jersey they score 5. In Illinois, Kentucky, Mississippi, and New Mexico legal corruption is perceived to be common not only in the executive and legislative branches but also in the judicial branch.

Executive Branch

In more than ten states legal corruption in executive branches is perceived to be "very common" or "extremely common." Georgia, Kentucky and New Jersey, for example, suffer from not only illegal corruption but also legal corruption. Executive branches in these states score 4 or higher in both forms of corruption. In Kansas, Maryland, Maine, North Carolina, New York, Ohio, and South Carolina, on the other hand, while illegal corruption in the executive branches is perceived to be "slightly common" or "not at all common," legal corruption is perceived to be "very common" or "extremely common." Most of the states in which the executive branches are perceived to be corrupt also led the nation in television ad spending (all donors) on gubernatorial races that were extremely competitive in 2014. In Connecticut, candidates spent approximately $12.50 per eligible voter (more than $25 million total); in Illinois, $10 ($75.5 million total); and in Florida, $8.50 (close $100 million total). In Colorado, which is perceived to be one of the less corrupt states, on the other hand, television ad spending was only $4.5 per eligible voter (11.5 million total) although the race was extremely competitive.[11]

Legislative Branch

Legal corruption in the legislative branch is particularly worrying in almost all states. In almost half of the states, it is perceived to be

either "very common" or "extremely common." Only in a few states do legislative branches score 2 or less. Kansas, Maryland, North Carolina, Nevada and Wisconsin suffer from only legal corruption, while a dozen states including Alabama, Illinois, Kentucky and New York, in which legal corruption is perceived to be "extremely common," suffer from both forms of corruption. In one state senate district in Nevada, for example, special interest groups spent close to $15 per eligible voter (more than $1.5 million) for television ads in 2014. In the entire state of Vermont, the total amount spent in the gubernatorial and lieutenant gubernatorial races was less than $1 million ($2 per eligible voter).[12]

Judicial Branch

Legal corruption in the judicial branch is more common than illegal corruption. Legal corruption in the judiciary is perceived to be more than "slightly common" in ten states and "very common" in Nevada, a non-partisan election state. Not surprisingly, states such as Alabama, Illinois, New Mexico, and Pennsylvania, which hold partisan elections to elect judges at all levels, score 3. Among the states that hold partisan elections, only in Texas is legal corruption in the judicial branch perceived to be "slightly common." Judicial branches in Georgia, Wisconsin, and West Virginia, which elect their judges via non-partisan elections, score higher than 2. The majority of the states in which legal corruption in the judicial branch is perceived be "not at all common" elect their judges via merit selection. In Illinois (a partisan election state), in a retention election for one Supreme Court seat, television ad spending (only by special interest groups) per eligible voter in 2014 was twice as much as a contested election for two seats together in Michigan (a non-partisan election state) in which legal corruption in the judicial branch is perceived to be "not at all common."[13]

Aggregating the Results: Most and Least Corrupt States

What are the most and least corrupt states, taking all three government branches into account? Although there is always some information lost in aggregation, which is particularly important in the measurement of corruption, it is still an important question. We simply add the median scores of each government branch and calculate the aggregate score of a state. The data presents the states whose aggregate scores are in the highest (i.e., most corrupt) and lowest (i.e., least corrupt) quartiles. With respect to illegal corruption, Arizona is perceived to be the most corrupt state, followed by a second group of states, which includes California and Kentucky, and third group that includes Alabama, Illinois, and New Jersey. Idaho, Maine, Massachusetts, New Hampshire, the Dakotas, and Vermont are perceived to be the least corrupt states, followed by a second group of states that includes Michigan and Oregon. Kentucky is not only perceived to be *illegally corrupt* but also *legally corrupt*. With respect to legal corruption, Kentucky is the most corrupt state followed by Illinois and Nevada while Massachusetts is the least corrupt state followed Michigan, Oregon, and Vermont. It is all bad news for Alabama, Georgia, Illinois, Kentucky, New Mexico, New Jersey, and Pennsylvania as their aggregate scores are in the highest quartiles of both illegal and legal corruption. Not so bad news for the Dakotas, Idaho, Massachusetts, Michigan, Oregon, Vermont, and Wyoming, which are perceived least corrupt both *illegally* and *legally*.

Notes

1. United States Department of Justice, "Report to Congress on the Activities and Operations of the Public Integrity Section," 2012.

2. Richard T. Boylan and Cheryl X. Long, "Measuring Public Corruption in the American States: A Survey of State House Reporters," *State Politics & Policy Quarterly* 3.4 (2003): 420-438.

3. Eric B. Rasmusen, Manu Raghav and Mark J. Ramseyer, "Convictions versus Conviction Rates: The Prosecutor's Choice," *American Law and Economics Review* 11.1 (2009): 47-78.

4. James E. Alt and David D. Lassen, "Enforcement and Public Corruption: Evidence from the American States," *Journal of Law, Economics and Organization* 30.2 (2014): 306-338.

5. Sanford C. Gordon, "Assessing Partisan Bias in Federal Public Corruption Prosecutions," *American Political Science Review* 103.4 (2009): 534-554.

6. Eric M. Uslaner, *Corruption, Inequality, and the Rule of Law: The Bulging Pocket Makes the Easy Life* (Cambridge University Press, 2008).

7. Boylan and Long, "Measuring Public Corruption in the American States."

8. Louisiana is colored red in the maps.

9. Lawrence Lessig, "Foreword: Institutional Corruption Defined," *Journal of Law Medicine and Ethics* 41.3 (2013): 553-555.

10. See, e.g. Brennan Center for Justice, "National Survey: Super PACs, Corruption, and Democracy," New York University School of Law, 2012.

11. Based on the authors' calculations using Chris Zubak-Skees, "State Ad Wars Tracker," Center for Public Integrity, September 22, 2014.

12. Id.

13. Id.

See also: Government & Law, Michael Johnston, Oguzhan C. Dincer

5

When Is a Gift a Bribe?

Judy Nadler and Miriam Schulman

Judy Nadler is a senior fellow and Miriam Schulman is Communications Director at the Markkula Center for Applied Ethics.

According to this viewpoint, the main difference between a gift and a bribe is the potential expectation on the part of the giver of something of value being received in return. Because it is often impossible to determine the expectations of the giver, all federal, state, and local officials—both elected and appointed—are governed by rules restricting gifts. The authors break down the issues related to gifts in politics.

D efining gifts and bribes may seem like a simple-minded activity, but, try posing the question another way, and you will see why this is an important issue in government ethics: What is the difference between a gift and a bribe? A gift is something of value given without the expectation of return; a bribe is the same thing given in the hope of influence or benefit.

Because it is often impossible to determine the expectation of the giver, all federal, state, and local officials, both elected and appointed, are governed by rules restricting gifts. In some cases, gifts over a certain amount are disallowed; in others, they must simply be reported. These rules can vary significantly from locality

"Gifts and Bribes," by Judy Nadler and Miriam Schulman, Santa Clara University. Reprinted with permission of the Markkula Center for Applied Ethics at Santa Clara University (www.scu.edu/ethics).

to locality, indicating disparities in each legislature's understanding of when a gift becomes a bribe.

Gifts and bribes can be actual items, or they can be tickets to a sporting event, travel, rounds of golf, or restaurant meals.

In this context, it is well for government officials to remember the old saying "There's no such thing as a free lunch," or even a free pencil. While many scoff at the idea that a pencil or notepad from a developer may influence political decision making, one question needs to be answered: Why does the developer go to the trouble and expense of making these items?

To answer, we can look at analogous experience from another field. E. Haavi Morreim has studied the influence of drug company marketing on physicians' prescribing habits. Her observation: When you ask doctors whether this kind of drug marketing is effective, the answer is always the same: "It doesn't influence me at all. They're not going to buy my soul with a laser pointer." The truth is ... this kind of advertising is crucial to sales. A doctor is not going to prescribe something he or she has never heard of, and it's the drug representative's job to get the products' names in front of the physicians."

Similarly, a member of the zoning commission who has been keeping a notepad from XYZ Builders next to his phone will remember the company when XYZ brings a matter before the commission. While no one is suggesting legislation that would prevent doctors or government officials from accepting inexpensive doodads, ethical politicians will recognize that any gift from someone with business before him or her is intended to exert an influence.

What Do Gifts and Bribes Have to Do with Ethics?

Political decisions are supposed to be made on the merits of the case, not based on whether or not the decision maker has received a lovely case of wine from one of the parties. This is a simple matter of fairness. When decision makers take gifts, even if their votes

are not influenced, they give the appearance of being on the take, which undermines public confidence in government.

What Ethical Dilemmas Do Gifts and Bribes Present?

People do not go into government work to make a lot of money. Especially at the local level, elected officials may receive only token payment for the number of hours they put into the job. In this context, it is tempting to say that tickets to the local performing arts center or sporting arena are well-deserved perks of office. Some even argue that attending such events is part of the job and crucial to understanding the experience of citizens who use these venues.

On the other side, such gifts may well influence officials when they need to determine whether the performing arts center should expand or whether the arena can add retail outlets that local businesses oppose. Also, such gifts can create a slippery slope, with officials coming to expect VIP treatment and making local businesses feel coerced into offering it so that they can receive a fair hearing.

By the same token, it is incumbent upon businesses to comply with government regulations on gift giving. While it may be common in the private sector to acknowledge important customers with extravagant holiday gifts, this practice is disallowed in the public sphere; the gravel company that tries to reward the mayor of a city that has made a big purchase with 10 pounds of expensive chocolate simply puts the mayor in the awkward position of returning the gift.

6

Those with the Wealth Also Have the Power

G. William Domhoff

G. William Domhoff, PhD, is a distinguished professor emeritus and research professor of psychology and sociology at the University of California, Santa Cruz. He is a founding faculty member of UCSC's Cowell College.

The data presented in this viewpoint indicates that wealth is highly concentrated in relatively few hands in the United States. Defining power as having the ability to realize wishes or reach goals even in the face of opposition, the author finds that the same set of households that score highest on wealth also score high on other power indicators. Consequently, he concludes that the United States is a power pyramid: it's tough for the bottom 80 percent—maybe even bottom 90 percent—to get organized and exercise much power.

This document presents details on the *wealth and income distributions* in the United States and explains how we use these two distributions as power indicators. The most striking numbers on income inequality will come last, showing the dramatic change in the ratio of the average CEO's paycheck to that of the average factory worker over the past 40 years.

First, though, some definitions. Generally speaking, *wealth* is the value of everything a person or family owns, minus any debts. However, for purposes of studying the wealth distribution,

"Wealth, Income, and Power," by G. William Domhoff, WhoRulesAmerica.net. Reprinted by permission.

economists define wealth in terms of *marketable assets*, such as real estate, stocks, and bonds, leaving aside consumer durables like cars and household items because they are not as readily converted into cash and are more valuable to their owners for use purposes than they are for resale (see Wolff, 2004, p. 4, for a full discussion of these issues). Once the value of all marketable assets is determined, then all debts, such as home mortgages and credit card debts, are subtracted, which yields a person's net worth. In addition, economists use the concept of *financial wealth*—also referred to in this document as "non-home wealth"—which is defined as net worth minus net equity in owner-occupied housing. As Wolff (2004, p. 5) explains, "Financial wealth is a more 'liquid' concept than marketable wealth, since one's home is difficult to convert into cash in the short term. It thus reflects the resources that may be immediately available for consumption or various forms of investments."

We also need to distinguish wealth from *income*. Income is what people earn from work but also from dividends, interest, and any rents or royalties that are paid to them on properties they own. In theory, those who own a great deal of wealth may or may not have high incomes, depending on the returns they receive from their wealth, but in reality those at the very top of the wealth distribution usually have the most income. (But it's important to note that for the rich, most of that income does not come from "working": in 2008, only 19% of the income reported by the 13,480 individuals or families making over $10 million came from wages and salaries. See Norris, 2010, for more details.)

This document focuses on the "Top 1%" as a whole because that's been the traditional cut-off point for "the top" in academic studies and because it's easy for us to keep in mind that we are talking about one in a hundred. But it is also important to realize that the lower half of that top 1% has far less than those in the top half; in fact, both wealth and income are super-concentrated in the top 0.1%, which is just one in a thousand.

[…]

There's also some general information available on median income and percentage of people below the poverty line in 2010. As might be expected, most of the new information shows declines; in fact, a report from the Center for Economic and Policy Research (2011) concludes that the decade from 2000 to 2010 was a "lost decade" for most Americans.

One final general point before turning to the specifics. People who have looked at this document in the past often asked whether progressive taxation reduces some of the income inequality that exists before taxes are paid. The answer: not by much, if we count *all* of the taxes that people pay, from sales taxes to property taxes to payroll taxes (in other words, not just income taxes). And the top 1% of income earners actually pay a *smaller* percentage of their incomes to taxes than the 9% just below them. These findings are discussed in detail near the end of this document.

[...]

The Wealth Distribution

In the United States, wealth is highly concentrated in relatively few hands. As of 2013, the top 1% of households (the upper class) owned 36.7% of all privately held wealth, and the next 19% (the managerial, professional, and small business stratum) had 52.2%, which means that just 20% of the people owned a remarkable 89%, leaving only 11% of the wealth for the bottom 80% (wage and salary workers). In terms of financial wealth (total net worth minus the value of one's home), the top 1% of households had an even greater share: 42.8%.

In terms of types of financial wealth, in 2013 the top one percent of households had 49.8% of all privately held stock, 54.7% of financial securities, and 62.8% of business equity. The top ten percent had 84% to 94% of stocks, bonds, trust funds, and business equity and almost 80% of non-home real estate. Since financial wealth is what counts as far as the control of income-producing assets, we can say that just 10% of the people *own* the United States of America.

There is a perception that a large number of Americans own stock—through mutual funds, trusts, pensions, or direct purchase of shares. This is true to some extent: 46% of American households have direct or indirect investments in the stock market. But the top 10% of households own 81% of the total value of those investments (Wolff, 2014); the vast majority have relatively meager holdings.

Inheritance and Estate Taxes

Figures on inheritance tell much the same story. According to a study published by the Federal Reserve Bank of Cleveland, only 1.6% of Americans receive $100,000 or more in inheritance. Another 1.1% receive $50,000 to $100,000. On the other hand, 91.9% receive nothing (Kotlikoff & Gokhale, 2000). Thus, the attempt by ultra-conservatives to eliminate inheritance taxes—which they always call "death taxes" for P.R. reasons—would take a huge bite out of government revenues (an estimated $253 billion between 2012 and 2022) for the benefit of the heirs of the mere 0.6% of Americans whose death would lead to the payment of any estate taxes whatsoever (Citizens for Tax Justice, 2010b).

It is noteworthy that some of the richest people in the country oppose this ultra-conservative initiative, suggesting that this effort is driven by anti-government ideology. In other words, few of the ultra-conservative and libertarian activists behind the effort will benefit from it in any material way. However, a study (Kenny et al., 2006) of the *financial* support for eliminating inheritance taxes discovered that 18 super-rich families (mostly Republican financial donors, but a few who support Democrats) provide the anti-government activists with most of the money for this effort.

Actually, ultra-conservatives and their wealthy financial backers may not have to bother to eliminate what remains of inheritance taxes at the federal level. The rich already have a new way to avoid inheritance taxes forever—for generations and generations—thanks to bankers. After Congress passed a reform in 1986 making it impossible for a "trust" to skip a generation before paying inheritance taxes, bankers convinced legislatures in

many states to eliminate their "rules against perpetuities," which means that trust funds set up in those states can exist in perpetuity, thereby allowing the trust funds to own new businesses, houses, and much else for descendants of rich people, and even to allow the beneficiaries to avoid payments to creditors when in personal debt or sued for causing accidents and injuries. About $100 billion in trust funds has flowed into those states so far. You can read the details on these "dynasty trusts" (which could be the basis for an even more solidified "American aristocracy") in a *New York Times* opinion piece published in July 2010 by Boston College law professor Ray Madoff, who also has a book on this and other new tricks: *Immortality and the Law: The Rising Power of the American Dead* (Yale University Press, 2010).

Home Ownership and Wealth

For the vast majority of Americans, their homes are by far the most significant wealth they possess.

Black and Latino households are faring significantly worse overall, whether we are talking about income or net worth. In 2013, the average white household had more than 15 times as much total wealth as the average African-American or Latino household. If we exclude home equity from the calculations and consider only financial wealth, the ratios are more than 200:1. Extrapolating from these figures, we see that 65% of white families' wealth is in the form of their principal residence; for Blacks and Hispanics, the figures are close to 90%.

And for all Americans, things got worse during the "Great Recession": comparing the 2007 numbers to the 2013 numbers, we can see a huge loss in wealth—both housing and financial—for most families, making the gap between the rich and the rest of America even greater and increasing the number of households with *no* marketable assets from 18.6% to 21.8% (Wolff, 2012 & 2014).

Do Americans Know Their Country's Wealth Distribution

An interesting study (Norton & Ariely, 2010) reveals that Americans have no idea that the wealth distribution (defined for them in terms of "net worth") is as concentrated as it is. When shown three pie charts representing possible wealth distributions, 90% or more of the 5,522 respondents—whatever their gender, age, income level, or party affiliation—thought that the American wealth distribution most resembled one in which the top 20% has about 60% of the wealth. In fact, of course, the top 20% control 85% of the wealth.

Even more striking, they did not come close on the amount of wealth held by the bottom 40% of the population. It's a number I haven't even mentioned so far, and it's shocking: the lowest two quintiles hold just 0.3% of the wealth in the United States. Most people in the survey guessed the figure to be between 8% and 10%, and two dozen academic economists got it wrong too, by guessing about 2%—seven times too high. Those surveyed did have it about right for what the 20% in the middle have; it's at the top and the bottom that they don't have any idea of what's going on.

Americans from all walks of life were also united in their vision of what the "ideal" wealth distribution would be, which may come as an even bigger surprise than their shared misinformation on the actual wealth distribution. They said that the ideal wealth distribution would be one in which the top 20% owned between 30 and 40 percent of the privately held wealth, which is a far cry from the 85 percent that the top 20% actually own. They also said that the bottom 40%—that's 120 million Americans—should have between 25% and 30%, not the mere 8% to 10% they thought this group had, and far above the 0.3% they actually had. In fact, there's no country in the world that has a wealth distribution close to what Americans think is ideal when it comes to fairness. So maybe Americans are much more egalitarian than most of them realize about each other, at least in principle and before the rat race begins.

Historical Context

Numerous studies show that the wealth distribution has been concentrated throughout American history, with the top 1% already owning 40-50% in large port cities like Boston, New York, and Charleston in the 1800s. (But it wasn't as bad in the 18th and 19th centuries as it is now, as summarized in a 2012 article in *The Atlantic.*) The wealth distribution was fairly stable over the course of the 20th century, although there were small declines in the aftermath of the New Deal and World II, when most people were working and could save a little money. There were progressive income tax rates, too, which took some money from the rich to help with government services.

Then there was a further decline, or flattening, in the 1970s, but this time in good part due to a fall in stock prices, meaning that the rich lost some of the value in their stocks. By the late 1980s, however, the wealth distribution was almost as concentrated as it had been in 1929, when the top 1% had 44.2% of all wealth. It has continued to edge up since that time, with a slight decline from 1998 to 2001, before the economy crashed in the late 2000s and little people got pushed down again.

Here are some dramatic facts that sum up how the wealth distribution became even more concentrated between 1983 and 2004, in good part due to the tax cuts for the wealthy and the defeat of labor unions: Of all the new financial wealth created by the American economy in that 21-year period, fully 42% of it went to the top 1%. A whopping 94% went to the top 20%, which of course means that the bottom 80% received only 6% of all the new financial wealth generated in the United States during the '80s, '90s, and early 2000s (Wolff, 2007).

The Rest of the World

Thanks to a 2006 study by the World Institute for Development Economics Research—using statistics for the year 2000—we now have information on the wealth distribution for the world as a whole, which can be compared to the United States and other

well-off countries. The authors of the report admit that the quality of the information available on many countries is very spotty and probably off by several percentage points, but they compensate for this problem with very sophisticated statistical methods and the use of different sets of data. With those caveats in mind, we can still safely say that the top 10% of the world's adults control about 85% of global household wealth—defined very broadly as all assets (not just financial assets), minus debts. That compares with a figure of 69.8% for the top 10% for the United States. The only industrialized democracy with a higher concentration of wealth in the top 10% than the United States is Switzerland at 71.3%.

The Relationship Between Wealth and Power

What's the relationship between wealth and power? To avoid confusion, let's be sure we understand they are two different issues. Wealth, as I've said, refers to the value of everything people own, minus what they owe, but the focus is on "marketable assets" for purposes of economic and power studies. Power, as explained elsewhere on this site, has to do with the ability (or call it capacity) to realize wishes, or reach goals, which amounts to the same thing, even in the face of opposition (Russell, 1938; Wrong, 1995). Some definitions refine this point to say that power involves Person A or Group A affecting Person B or Group B "in a manner contrary to B's interests," which then necessitates a discussion of "interests," and quickly leads into the realm of philosophy (Lukes, 2005, p. 30). Leaving those discussions for the philosophers, at least for now, how do the concepts of wealth and power relate?

First, wealth can be seen as a "resource" that is very useful in exercising power. That's obvious when we think of donations to political parties, payments to lobbyists, and grants to experts who are employed to think up new policies beneficial to the wealthy. Wealth also can be useful in shaping the general social environment to the benefit of the wealthy, whether through hiring public relations firms or donating money for universities, museums, music halls, and art galleries.

Second, certain kinds of wealth, such as stock ownership, can be used to control corporations, which of course have a major impact on how the society functions.

Third, just as wealth can lead to power, so too can power lead to wealth. Those who control a government can use their position to feather their own nests, whether that means a favorable land deal for relatives at the local level or a huge federal government contract for a new corporation run by friends who will hire you when you leave government. If we take a larger historical sweep and look cross-nationally, we are well aware that the leaders of conquering armies often grab enormous wealth and that some religious leaders use their positions to acquire wealth.

There's a fourth way that wealth and power relate. For research purposes, the wealth distribution can be seen as the main "value distribution" within the general power indicator I call "who benefits." What follows in the next three paragraphs is a little long-winded, I realize, but it needs to be said because some social scientists—primarily pluralists—argue that who wins and who loses in a variety of policy conflicts is the only valid power indicator (Dahl, 1957, 1958; Polsby, 1980). And philosophical discussions don't even mention wealth or other power indicators (Lukes, 2005).

Here's the argument: if we assume that most people would like to have as great a share as possible of the things that are valued in the society, then we can infer that those who have the most goodies are the most powerful. Although some value distributions may be unintended outcomes that do not really reflect power, as pluralists are quick to tell us, the general distribution of valued experiences and objects within a society still can be viewed as the most publicly visible and stable outcome of the operation of power.

In American society, for example, wealth and well-being are highly valued. People seek to own property, to have high incomes, to have interesting and safe jobs, to enjoy the finest in travel and leisure, and to live long and healthy lives. All of these "values" are unequally distributed, and all may be utilized as power indicators.

However, the primary focus with this type of power indicator is on the wealth distribution sketched out in the previous section.

The argument for using the wealth distribution as a power indicator is strengthened by studies showing that such distributions vary historically and from country to country, depending upon the relative strength of rival political parties and trade unions, with the United States having the most highly concentrated wealth distribution of any Western democracy except Switzerland. For example, in a study based on 18 Western democracies, strong trade unions and successful social democratic parties correlated with greater equality in the income distribution and a higher level of welfare spending (Stephens, 1979).

And now we have arrived at the point I want to make. If the top 1% of households have 30-35% of the wealth, that's 30 to 35 times what they would have if wealth were equally distributed, and so we infer that they must be powerful. And then we set out to see if the same set of households scores high on other power indicators (it does). Next we study how that power operates, which is what most articles on this site are about. Furthermore, if the top 20% have 84% of the wealth (and recall that 10% have 85% to 90% of the stocks, bonds, trust funds, and business equity), that means that the United States is a power pyramid. It's tough for the bottom 80%—maybe even the bottom 90%—to get organized and exercise much power.

Income and Power

The income distribution also can be used as a power indicator. As Table 7 shows, it is not as concentrated as the wealth distribution, but the top 1% of income earners did receive 17.2% of all income in 2009. That's up from 12.8% for the top 1% in 1982, which is quite a jump, and it parallels what is happening with the wealth distribution. This is further support for the inference that the power of the corporate community and the upper class have been increasing in recent decades.

The rising concentration of income can be seen in a special *New York Times* analysis by David Cay Johnston of an Internal

Revenue Service report on income in 2004. Although overall income had grown by 27% since 1979, 33% of the gains went to the top 1%. Meanwhile, the bottom 60% were making less: about 95 cents for each dollar they made in 1979. The next 20%—those between the 60th and 80th rungs of the income ladder—made $1.02 for each dollar they earned in 1979. Furthermore, Johnston concludes that only the top 5% made significant gains ($1.53 for each 1979 dollar). Most amazing of all, the top 0.1%—that's one-tenth of one percent—had more combined pre-tax income than the poorest 120 million people (Johnston, 2006).

But the increase in what is going to the few at the top did not level off, even with all that. As of 2007, income inequality in the United States was at an all-time high for the past 95 years, with the top 0.01%—that's one-hundredth of one percent—receiving 6% of all US wages, which is double what it was for that tiny slice in 2000; the top 10% received 49.7%, the highest since 1917 (Saez, 2009). However, in an analysis of 2008 tax returns for the top 0.2%— that is, those whose income tax returns reported $1,000,000 or more in income (mostly from individuals, but nearly a third from couples)—it was found that they received 13% of all income, down slightly from 16.1% in 2007 due to the decline in payoffs from financial assets (Norris, 2010).

And the rate of increase is even higher for the very richest of the rich: the top 400 income earners in the United States. According to another analysis by Johnston (2010a), the average income of the top 400 tripled during the Clinton Administration and doubled during the first seven years of the Bush Administration. So by 2007, the top 400 averaged $344.8 million per person, up 31% from an average of $263.3 million just one year earlier. (For another recent revealing study by Johnston, read "Is Our Tax System Helping Us Create Wealth?")

How are these huge gains possible for the top 400? It's due to cuts in the tax rates on capital gains and dividends, which were down to a mere 15% in 2007 thanks to the tax cuts proposed by the Bush Administration and passed by Congress in 2003. Since

almost 75% of the income for the top 400 comes from capital gains and dividends, it's not hard to see why tax cuts on income sources available to only a tiny percent of Americans mattered greatly for the high-earning few. Overall, the *effective* tax rate on high incomes fell by 7% during the Clinton presidency and 6% in the Bush era, so the top 400 had a tax rate of 20% or less in 2007, far lower than the marginal tax rate of 35% that the highest income earners (over $372,650) supposedly pay. It's also worth noting that only the first $106,800 of a person's income is taxed for Social Security purposes (as of 2010), so it would clearly be a boon to the Social Security Fund if everyone—not just those making less than $106,800—paid the Social Security tax on their full incomes.

[...]

Income Ratios and Power: Executives vs. Average Workers

Another way that income can be used as a power indicator is by comparing average CEO annual pay to average factory worker pay, something that has been done for many years by *Business Week* and, later, the Associated Press. The ratio of CEO pay to factory worker pay rose from 42:1 in 1960 to as high as 531:1 in 2000, at the height of the stock market bubble, when CEOs were cashing in big stock options. It was at 411:1 in 2005 and 344:1 in 2007, according to research by United for a Fair Economy. By way of comparison, the same ratio is about 25:1 in Europe.

It's even more revealing to compare the actual rates of increase of the salaries of CEOs and ordinary workers; from 1990 to 2005, CEOs' pay increased almost 300% (adjusted for inflation), while production workers gained a scant 4.3%. The purchasing power of the federal minimum wage actually *declined* by 9.3%, when inflation is taken into account.

Although some of the information I've relied upon to create this section on executives' vs. workers' pay is a few years old now, the AFL/CIO provides up-to-date information on CEO salaries at their Web site. There, you can learn that the median compensation

for CEOs in *all* industries as of early 2010 is $3.9 million; it's
$10.6 million for the companies listed in Standard and Poor's
500, and $19.8 million for the companies listed in the Dow-
Jones Industrial Average. Since the median worker's pay is about
$36,000, then you can quickly calculate that CEOs in general make
100 times as much as the workers, that CEOs of S&P 500 firms
make almost 300 times as much, and that CEOs at the Dow-Jones
companies make 550 times as much. (For a more recent update
on CEOs' pay, see "The Drought Is Over (At Least for CEOs)" at
NYTimes.com; the article reports that the median compensation
for CEOs at 200 major companies was $9.6 million in 2010—up
by about 12% over 2009 and generally equal to or surpassing pre-
recession levels. For specific information about some of the top
CEOs, see http://projects.nytimes.com/executive_compensation.

If you wonder how such a large gap could develop, the
proximate, or most immediate, factor involves the way in which
CEOs now are able to rig things so that the board of directors,
which they help select—and which includes some fellow CEOs on
whose boards they sit—gives them the pay they want. The trick is
in hiring outside experts, called "compensation consultants," who
give the process a thin veneer of economic respectability.

The process has been explained in detail by a retired CEO
of DuPont, Edgar S. Woolard, Jr., who is now chair of the New
York Stock Exchange's executive compensation committee. His
experience suggests that he knows whereof he speaks, and he speaks
because he's concerned that corporate leaders are losing respect
in the public mind. He says that the business page chatter about
CEO salaries being set by the competition for their services in the
executive labor market is "bull." As to the claim that CEOs deserve
ever higher salaries because they "create wealth," he describes that
rationale as a "joke," says the *New York Times* (Morgenson, 2005).

Here's how it works, according to Woolard:

> *The compensation committee [of the board of directors] talks
> to an outside consultant who has surveys you could drive a
> truck through and pay anything you want to pay, to be perfectly*

honest. The outside consultant talks to the human resources vice president, who talks to the CEO. The CEO says what he'd like to receive. It gets to the human resources person who tells the outside consultant. And it pretty well works out that the CEO gets what he's implied he thinks he deserves, so he will be respected by his peers. (Morgenson, 2005.)

The board of directors buys into what the CEO asks for because the outside consultant is an "expert" on such matters. Furthermore, handing out only modest salary increases might give the wrong impression about how highly the board values the CEO. And if someone on the board should object, there are the three or four CEOs from other companies who will make sure it happens. It is a process with a built-in escalator.

As for why the consultants go along with this scam, they know which side their bread is buttered on. They realize the CEO has a big say-so on whether or not they are hired again. So they suggest a package of salaries, stock options and other goodies that they think will please the CEO, and they, too, get rich in the process. And certainly the top executives just below the CEO don't mind hearing about the boss's raise. They know it will mean pay increases for them, too. (For an excellent detailed article on the main consulting firm that helps CEOs and other corporate executives raise their pay, check out the *New York Times* article entitled "America's Corporate Pay Pal," which supports everything Woolard of DuPont claim and adds new information.)

If hiring a consulting firm doesn't do the trick as far as raising CEO pay, then it may be possible for the CEO to have the board change the way in which the success of the company is determined. For example, Walmart Stores, Inc. used to link the CEO's salary to sales figures at established stores. But when declining sales no longer led to big pay raises, the board simply changed the magic formula to use total companywide sales instead. By that measure, the CEO could still receive a pay hike (Morgenson, 2011).

There's a much deeper power story that underlies the self-dealing and mutual back-scratching by CEOs now carried out

through interlocking directorates and seemingly independent outside consultants. It probably involves several factors. At the least, on the workers' side, it reflects their loss of power following the all-out attack on unions in the 1960s and 1970s, which is explained in detail in an excellent book by James Gross (1995), a labor and industrial relations professor at Cornell. That decline in union power made possible and was increased by both outsourcing at home and the movement of production to developing countries, which were facilitated by the break-up of the New Deal coalition and the rise of the New Right (Domhoff, 1990, Chapter 10). It signals the shift of the United States from a high-wage to a low-wage economy, with professionals protected by the fact that foreign-trained doctors and lawyers aren't allowed to compete with their American counterparts in the direct way that low-wage foreign-born workers are.

On the other side of the class divide, the rise in CEO pay may reflect the increasing power of chief executives as compared to major owners and stockholders in general, not just their increasing power over workers. CEOs may now be the center of gravity in the corporate community and the power elite, displacing the leaders in wealthy owning families (e.g., the second and third generations of the Walton family, the owners of Walmart). True enough, the CEOs are sometimes ousted by their generally go-along boards of directors, but they are able to make hay and throw their weight around during the time they are king of the mountain.

The claims made in the previous paragraph need much further investigation. But they demonstrate the ideas and research directions that are suggested by looking at the wealth and income distributions as indicators of power.

7

Wealth Inequality Data Is Nonsense

Scott Sumner

Scott Sumner taught economics at Bentley University between 1982 and 2015. He is currently director of the Program on Monetary Policy at the Mercatus Center.

The author makes the case that data on inequality of income and wealth is flawed because capital income is nothing like wage income, and it is actually deferred consumption. Further, this flaw makes conclusions about economic inequality based on the available data false to the point of nonsense. Instead, Sumner suggests that we look at qualitative data on how Americans live rather than quantitative data to get a better sense of whether income inequality is an issue.

I keep running across blog posts showing the inequality of income and wealth in America. In a recent post I already discussed one reason why this data is fatally flawed, capital income is nothing like wage income—rather it is deferred consumption. Counting capital income and wage income is actually counting the same income twice. Here I'd like to discuss some other problems with the data:

- Life Cycle Effects: I dragged out my annual Social Security data that I get in the mail, and it shows how much I earned during each year. I tried to do a rough adjustment for cost of living changes, to make things fairer (otherwise my income

"Income and wealth inequality data: Nonsense on stilts," TheMoneyIllusion. Reprinted by permission.

looks extremely unequal.) I am pretty sure my five income "quintiles" are roughly as follows: 3%, 13%, 22%, 27%, and 35%. In other words during my worst 7 years I made 3% of my total real lifetime income, and during my best 5 years about 35%. Some people have a more equal profile, whereas others have a far more unequal profile. I think I'm probably not that atypical. The point is that if we had 100% lifetime equality in earnings, but wages that rose with age and experience, then that's the sort of income inequality we might observe in America. The actual income inequality is greater, because inequality is not just due to life-cycle effects.

- Inflation: Suppose you are the richest guy in the world, owning $100 billion in Microsoft stock. You cash out and decide to live off the interest. To avoid inflation risk, you put it all in 10-year indexed TIPS. You would earn $650,000,000 per year in interest. Unfortunately your tax liability would be more than $650,000,000. The government would report your income as about $2 billion. So the person who might well have the highest reported income in the entire country according to official data might not have any real income at all. Now obviously most rich people don't put all their money in TIPS. They take bigger risks and get positive rates of return. But risk implies the possibility of loss. Some do much worse than the hypothetical I gave you. Of course even with no income a person this rich has a fabulous lifestyle, which is what I would argue is exactly the point. Look at consumption inequality, not income inequality.

- I am pretty sure that a lot of the wealth inequality data is incomplete. I recall reading that it often ignores structures (which is much of the wealth for average homeowners and shopkeepers.) It may ignore pensions. Many retired public employees have defined benefit pensions that would be hard to replicate with a 401k holding a million dollars. It

ignores human capital, making it impossible to compare human capital-rich brain surgeons and lawyers with physical capital-rich farmers and landlords.

- Income inequality data is often collected at the household level, implying that a doctor making $250,000 with a stay at home spouse is no better off than a Boston cop making $150,000 (including lots of overtime) married to a nurse making $100,000 (including lots of overtime). But the two-income couple might have to spend money on child care and have very stressful lives doing household chores on top of their paid jobs. This isn't a major bias, but many people who naively think of the top quintile as being "rich" would be shocked at how many working class couples in their 40s or 50s who are dual income and live in high-cost areas like NYC and Boston actually fall into that category. I'd guess two married people each making $55,000 would make it the top quintile, and I'd guess a couple who each make $75,000 would make the top decile. Those aren't gaudy incomes around here.

I am not trying to argue the upper middle class can't afford to pay more taxes. (I don't want to get mauled like that poor U of C professor.) Indeed, I think most Americans could afford to pay much more taxes, as we've become used to having lots of stuff we really don't need. A small Hyundai will get us from A to B just as well as a Lexus. So that's not the point.

Instead, my point is that we should ignore all the official data, and use our eyes. Travel around the country. Go into poor people's houses. In the 1970s I recall staying with a rural family of six in a small house who had running water for only a couple hours of the day. Over the course of my life I've seen lots of poor urban and rural neighborhoods. And I've driven around affluent areas like Newport Beach and Wellesey and very rich areas like Beverly Hills. I don't really know what's it's like to be poor in a cultural sense, or not be able to afford food for my family, but I think I do have a rough sense of the different sorts of consumption bundles

purchased by different classes of people. For what it's worth, here's my impressions:

- All classes in America are better off than in the 1960s. But the gains are most noticeable for the poor and rich. Especially the poor in the rural South.
- The US has more inequality than other developed countries.
- Some income redistribution should occur, via a progressive consumption tax and subsidies for the poor (wages subsidies, disability subsidies, HSA subsidies, education vouchers, etc.).

So I don't have any objection to policies of redistribution, which is what motivates all these comparisons. But it annoys me that people are making arguments using worthless data.

It shows wealth inequality by quintile, using data that is utterly meaningless, then shows wealth inequality as perceived by the average American. Here you are supposed to laugh at the stupidity of Americans. But their view may actually be closer to the truth than the official data. Then the graph shows the inequality that Americans think would be fair. Even the Bush voters opt for a wealth distribution far more equal than what we actually have.

Here's the problem with this entire enterprise. Let's work with the wealth definition that was probably used in this data, that is, only easy to measure financial assets. Assume this data is correct. How much income equality would we need to get things as equal as the Bush voters want? I'm going to claim that even 100% income equality would not be enough. That's right, if you paid a 16-year-old boy with pimples at McDonalds exactly the same income as a brain surgeon at Mass General, *measured wealth in America would still be far more unequal that what Bush voters say we should aim for.* That makes Bush voters to the left of Mao, almost at Pol Pot levels of egalitarianism. And the reason is simple. Even with exactly equal incomes, people will vary greatly in how much they save and how well they invest what they do save. So even

with equal incomes, some would become very wealthy, and some would save almost nothing.

With apologies to Bentham, income inequality data is nonsense, and wealth inequality data is nonsense on stilts. It's all about consumption.

Yglesias' post was entitled "Poor People Are Much Poorer Than You Think." Actually, if you are an observant person, and ignore the data, economic inequality in America is exactly what you'd think.

8

Unleashed Campaign Spending Thanks to *Citizens United*

Gary Beckner and Richard Posner

Beginning in 2004, Nobel Prize–winning economist Gary S. Becker and renowned jurist and legal scholar Richard A. Posner wrote and shared the Becker-Posner Blog. The blog was discontinued in 2014 with Becker's passing.

Donations to political campaigns have long been regulated due to the fear that unlimited donations could corrupt the political process. A large amount of money is likely to have strings, or at least expectations, attached. According to the US Supreme Court's Citizens United *decision, the risk of corruption would be slight if the donor were not contributing to a candidate or a political party but merely expressing his political preferences through an independent organization such as a super PAC. The authors of this viewpoint think differently.*

The Supreme Court's 2010 decision in *Citizens United v. Federal Election Commission* held that Congress cannot limit expenditures in political campaigns as long as the spender, who might be an individual or an organization, including a corporation or union, is not affiliated with or acting in concert with the candidate or political party. The Court held that such "independent" expenditures are not campaign donations, which

"Unlimited Campaign Spending—A Good Thing? Posner," by Gary Beckner and Richard Posner, The Becker-Posner Blog, April 8, 2012. Reprinted by permission.

can be regulated; they are pure expressions of the political preferences of the donors.

Some of the expenditures are made directly by donors to buy political advertising, but most (84 percent of the roughly $100 million in such "independent" expenditures already made in the current presidential primary campaign) are given by the donors to political action committees (called "super PACs"), which channel the expenditures into political ads or other methods of influencing political opinion. This is sensible intermediation since the donors are unlikely to be knowledgeable about creating or buying or placing ads.

The Supreme Court allows donations to political campaigns to be regulated (and limited) because of fear that donations unlimited in amount corrupt the political process, because the candidate recipient knows that a donor of a large amount of money expects something in return, usually favorable consideration of a policy that would benefit the donor, and hence a large donation is likely to be a tacit bribe. But the Court, rather naively as it seems to most observers, reasoned in the *Citizens United* case that the risk of corruption would be slight if the donor was not contributing to a candidate or a political party but merely expressing his political preferences through an independent organization such as a super PAC—an organization neither controlled by nor even coordinating with a candidate or political party.

The criticisms of the Court's reasoning are several. First, the notion of "coordination" is vague, and tacit coordination with a candidate or a party seems to occupy the same never-never land as tacit collusion in antitrust law. It can be quite effective yet is hard to condemn as actual coordination. Allies of the candidate or members of the party can run the super PAC and without even talking to the candidate or to party officials can figure out what kind of political advertising will be helpful to the candidate. Most super PAC advertising has been negative—that is, has attacked opponents of the candidate whom the super PAC favors—because positive advertising would be difficult without explicit coordination; the

reason is that candidates tend to be vague and protean about what they favor, in order to maintain their freedom of action and reaction, so a super PAC could operate at cross-purposes with its favored candidate if it advertised in support of a program that it thought the candidate would favor. In addition, negative political advertising is usually more effective than positive.

It thus is difficult to see what practical difference there is between super PAC donations and direct campaign donations, from a corruption standpoint. A super PAC is a valuable weapon for a campaign, as the heavy expenditures of Restore Our Future, the large super PAC that supports Romney and has attacked his opponents, proves; the donors to it are known; and it is unclear why they should expect less quid pro quo from their favored candidate if he's successful than a direct donor to the candidate's campaign would be.

So the real question is whether campaign donations, in whatever guise, should be limited. There are two arguments. The first and less is that, as with brand advertising, advertising pro and con competing politicians tends to be offsetting; the argument is that if the contestants' spending is limited, this will not affect the outcome of the contest but merely reduce its cost. But the argument is weak because it fails to account for the need of a new entrant to spend more heavily than incumbents in order to offset the cumulative effect of earlier expenditures. Even if the producer of some famous brand stopped advertising altogether, it would be years before consumers began to forget about the brand and stop buying it, but a new entrant would have no existing body of consumer good will to fall back on.

The stronger argument for limiting campaign donations is the corruption argument, which I have just suggested is as strong against the super PACs as it is against direct campaign donations. But again there is the concern with new entrants. If a candidate's name is Bush or Clinton or Kennedy (and he or she is related to a former President who bore one of those names), the candidate enters a political campaign with an information advantage by virtue

of belonging to a well known political dynasty extending over two or more generations (hence like an established brand). An unknown may need to spend more than one of those dynasts to pull even. Yet it hardly seems feasible to fix a limit on contributions and then raise it for new entrants.

That said, I think the emergence of new media in the Internet era makes the corruption argument stronger than the new-entrant argument. The reason is that the Internet greatly reduces the expense of disseminating information, whether about a candidate or anything else. The number of over the air radio and television stations is limited and likewise the number of newspapers and magazines, but nowadays most people are getting their information, including political information, from social media, blogs, tweets, and other modes of communication, effectively infinite in number, accessible costly over cell phones, laptops, and other electronic devices. These technologies for creating, disseminating, and receiving information at very low cost should enable any candidate with a persuasive message to reach a large audience of potential voters and should thus favor new entrants in political as in other markets—provided they are not allowed to be drowned by enormous expenditures by super PACs.

We saw the effect of the new information technologies at work in the 2008 Democratic primary season, when the relatively unknown Barack Obama defeated the much better known Hillary Clinton, and we have seen it again and more dramatically (consistent with the rapid expansion and adoption of these technologies) in the current Republican primary campaign. Michelle Bachman, Herman Cain, Rick Perry, Ron Paul, and Rick Santorum, none of whom was nationally prominent (Santorum had once been, but after his one-sided defeat for reelection to the Senate in 2006 had lapsed into obscurity), were able to compete effectively with the better-known candidates (Romney and Gingrich) and lost because of lack of support rather than lack of campaign funds. True, Santorum and Gingrich were both bolstered by super PACs,

but they were hammered by Restore Our Future, thus providing a good example of offsetting "arms race" political expenditures.

But could it be that the more that is spent on political campaigns, the more informed the voting public becomes? This suggestion is hard to take seriously. Political candidates seem to have a very condescending view of the American electorate; almost no information is conveyed by political advertising. Debates and other campaign appearances provide voters with insights into the character and intelligence of candidates, but positive political advertising is largely a mode of hagiography, and negative of defamation.

9

How *Citizens United* Changed the Rules of the Game

Represent.Us

Represent.Us is a not-for-profit organization that brings together people across the political spectrum to pass powerful anti-corruption laws to stop bribery, end secret money, and fix broken elections.

The US Supreme Court's Citizens United *decision did not change the limits on campaign contributions made directly to candidates, but it did lift the limits on contributions made to Political Action Committees (PACs), which is considered independent political spending. The unlimited amounts of money pouring into the new "super PACs" can't contribute directly to a candidate's campaign, but they can certainly make a huge impact nonetheless. The viewpoint discusses the role of PACs and Super PACs in campaigns.*

"Citizens United" is shorthand for a landmark 2010 Supreme Court case—*Citizens United v. FEC*—that changed the face of campaign finance and money in politics in the United States.

Citizens United overturned certain long-standing restrictions on political fundraising and spending—transforming the entire political landscape of the country.

Most notably, *Citizens United* granted corporations, nonprofits, and unions unlimited political spending power.

"What is Citizens United?" Represent.Us. https://represent.us/action/citizens-united-2-2/. Licensed under CC BY 3.0 US.

What's a PAC Got to Do with It?

Contrary to popular belief, *Citizens United* didn't change the contribution limits on candidates' official campaign funds. The laws *Citizens United* overturned were about *independent political spending*—the kind of spending done by PACs (Political Action Committees).

PACs are independent groups created to raise money to support a particular candidate. Any individual or group can form a PAC. Traditional PACs can donate directly to a candidate's campaign fund. PACs also generate their own "electioneering media"—like those ubiquitous TV ads promoting or attacking a candidate.

Before *Citizens United* there were limits on how much money individuals could contribute to PACs, and corporations, unions, and certain types of nonprofits weren't allowed to give to PACs at all.

Then *Citizens United* came along and changed the rules of the game.

What Exactly Did *Citizens United* Do?

Citizens United lifted the limits on how much individuals can contribute to PACs and allowed corporations, non-profit groups, and unions to give to PACs for the first time (also in unlimited amounts).

The result? A tidal wave of money flooded subsequent elections. For the first time in history, anyone—and any group—could spend unlimited amounts of money promoting a political candidate via super PACs.

It's important to understand we're not talking about unlimited campaign contributions here. *Citizens United* impacted *independent political spending* only.

A candidate's official campaign is a whole other animal. PACs are not supposed to coordinate with candidates' campaigns at all. (In reality, they do all the time, but that's another story).

What's the Difference Between a PAC and a Super PAC?

The new rules put in place by *Citizens United* allowed for the creation of a new kind of PAC known as a "super PAC."

Super PACs can raise unlimited amounts of money and can accept unlimited contributions from corporations, non-profit groups, and unions.

Unlike traditional PACs, however, super PACs can't contribute funds directly to the candidate's campaign.

Why Did *Citizens United* Happen?

The funny thing about *Citizens United v. FEC* is that the case started off as no big deal.

In the heat of the 2008 presidential election, a conservative PAC called "Citizens United" wanted to air a pay-per-view film it produced that was critical of Hillary Clinton. But a law enforced by the Federal Election Commission (FEC) barred paid television broadcasts about individual candidates right before primaries and elections. The FEC wouldn't allow Citizens United to run its film.

So Citizens United sued the FEC in a lawsuit called "*Citizens United v. FEC*." (Hence the eventual shorthand for the case, *Citizens United*).

The people behind the Citizens United PAC weren't trying to overhaul the country's campaign finance laws. They were just arguing that the FEC restrictions on TV ads shouldn't apply to their Hillary pay-per-view film.

The lower court where their case originated ruled against them, so Citizens United took its case all the way to the Supreme Court.

The Supreme Court Justices who ruled on the case could have given Citizens United everything it was asking for, without changing any laws, by ruling narrowly that the electioneering media restrictions didn't apply to the Citizens United PAC's pay-per-view video about Hillary.

But instead, the Supreme Court overturned long-standing campaign finance laws, dramatically changing how elections are funded in the United States.

So what happened? Good question.

Some blame it on a blunder by the FEC's lawyer. A Justice asked him if current law could theoretically prevent publication of books by political advocacy organizations in time periods preceding elections. He answered a conditional "Yes," and set off free speech alarm bells. Big time.

Others say the Justices reigning at the time wanted to change the laws and they used the case as an excuse to do so.

What's the Argument in Favor of *Citizens United*?

The Supreme Court Justices who voted in favor of the *Citizens United* ruling argued that prohibiting or limiting independent expenditures by corporations and certain types of groups violates Americans' First Amendment right to free speech.

This argument rests on two prior court cases. The first, *First National Bank v. Belloti*, decided that, as associations of citizens, corporations have a right to free speech (i.e. "corporations are people"). The second, *Buckley v. Valeo*, decided that spending money to influence elections is a form of constitutionally protected free speech (i.e. "money is speech").

The logic goes like this: if corporations have a right to free speech, and free speech includes spending money, then preventing corporations from spending money on political speech violates the First Amendment.

> "If the First Amendment has any force, it prohibits Congress from fining or jailing citizens, or associations of citizens, for simply engaging in political speech." –Justice Kennedy

What's the Argument Against *Citizens United*?

The four Justices who opposed *Citizens United*, fervently led by Justice Stevens, argued that corporate entities are not "We the People for whom our Constitution was established," and

therefore should not be given free speech protections under the First Amendment.

They argued that corporations can unfairly influence elections with vast sums of money few individuals can match, distorting the public debate, and potentially leading to corruption or the appearance of corruption.

Because the Constitution allows the government to prevent corruption, the dissenting Justices held that corporate political expenses should be regulated. They argued that the unique qualities of corporations and other artificial entities make them dangerous to democratic elections and that the distorting and corrupting influence of a dominant funding source is a constitutional reason to regulate corporate political spending.

Justice Stevens also asserted that, in their ruling, the Majority Justices addressed a question not raised by the original case and "changed the case to give themselves an opportunity to change the laws."

> "A democracy cannot function effectively when its constituent members believe laws are being bought and sold." –Justice Stevens

Did *Citizens United* Make Money=Free Speech?

No. The idea that money=free speech was established in a court case called *Buckley v. Valeo*. In this case, the Court ruled that spending money to influence elections is a form of free speech and therefore protected by the First Amendment.

Citizens United relied on the principle of "money=free speech" but did not establish it.

Did *Citizens United* Create Corporate Personhood?

No. Many people mistakenly think that *Citizens United* created the idea that "corporations are people" and are therefore protected by the First Amendment right to free speech. Actually, that idea was first established in a previous court case known as *Belloti* (shorthand for *First National Bank of Boston v. Belloti)*, which

defined corporations as having a right to free speech for the first time.

Citizens United relied on the idea of "corporate personhood" but did not establish it.

What If We Could Overturn *Citizens United*?

If we overturned *Citizens United*, we'd be rid of super PACs, and independent political expenditures would be regulated again. But America would still face a huge corruption problem.

Overturning *Citizens United* would turn back the campaign finance clock to 2010. But that's about it. America's political system is broken—and the problem runs deeper than *Citizens United*.

Lobbyists are writing laws and effectively bribing legislators. Legislators are turning around and becoming lobbyists. And—super PACs or no—candidates' campaigns are being funded by a tiny slice of Americans.

The Good News? We Can Beat Corruption Even Without Overturning *Citizens United*

Hoping Washington will reform itself is like asking the fox to lock up the henhouse. Instead of waiting on Congress, we can go around it.

In cities and states across the country, people are passing laws based on model legislation called The American Anti-Corruption Act. These laws go beyond what overturning *Citizens United* would do, enacting broad-based reforms to stop political bribery, end secret money, and give voters a stronger voice. And—like many other grassroots campaigns that have ended up changing federal laws—the momentum is building towards a federal victory.

Congress isn't going to fix this for us. Neither is the Supreme Court. It's up to us, everyday Americans, to fix our broken political system. That's how all good things have come about in this country, right? That's what we, the people, are all about.

10

Comments on the Deeply Flawed US Electoral System

Andrew Gumbel

Andrew Gumbel is a Los Angeles-based journalist and author whose most recent book, Down for the Count: Dirty Elections and the Rotten History of Democracy in America, *was published in 2016.*

US election experts and voting rights activists believe Kris Kobach, vice-chair of the Presidential Advisory Commission on Election Integrity, is intent on instituting a sweeping wave of new voter suppression laws. The authors suggest that the politics of electoral combat have been heating towards boiling point for a decade and a half. They assert that this is the product of a political system that has never, in more than two centuries, resolved basic questions of democratic accountability.

When Kris Kobach was first running for office in Kansas in 2010, he claimed he'd found evidence that thousands of Kansans were assuming the identities of dead voters and casting fraudulent ballots—a technique once known as ghost voting.

Kobach even offered a name, Albert K Brewer of Wichita, who he said had voted from beyond the grave in the primaries that year.

But then it emerged that Albert K Brewer, aged 78, was still very much alive, a registered Republican like Kobach, and more than a

little stunned to be told he'd moved on to the great hereafter. No evidence emerged that anyone had ghost voted in Kansas that year.

Seven years on, as Donald Trump's point man on reforming the US electoral system, Kobach has not backed away from those same scare tactics—no matter that he is frequently called a fraud and a liar, and his allegations entirely baseless.

On the contrary. Backed by a president who, days after assuming office, claimed that 3 to 5 million fraudulent ballots had been cast for Hillary Clinton, Kobach is enthusiastically spreading stories of voter impersonation on a massive scale, of out-of-state students voting twice, and of non-citizens casting illegal ballots.

As vice-chair of the Presidential Advisory Commission on Election Integrity, his mission to root out "fraudulent voter registrations and fraudulent voting" is sending chills down the spines of election experts and voting rights activists who believe he is intent on instituting a sweeping wave of new voter suppression laws.

Vanita Gupta, who headed the justice department's civil rights division under President Obama, calls the commission "a pretext … to kick millions of eligible voters off the rolls and undermine the sanctity of our election systems." Already in conjunction with a commission hearing in New Hampshire on Tuesday, a Kobach ally proposed instituting a system of background checks on voters as strict as the checks liberal groups want to impose on gun buyers.

Kobach did not respond to an interview request from the *Guardian*.

While it may seem astonishing to see such tactics being deployed in the world's most powerful democracy, they cannot be attributed solely to the rise of Trump. In truth, the politics of electoral combat have been heating towards boiling point for a decade and a half—and are the product of a political system that has never, in more than two centuries, resolved basic questions of democratic accountability and is thus unique in the developed western world.

The 2000 presidential election, and in particular the bruising 36-day fight over Florida's votes, exposed flaws in the US electoral system that many Americans had not thought about since the end of segregation and the landmark achievements of the civil rights era.

Not only was there a problem of reliability with the voting machines, it also became clear that the United States had never established an unequivocal right to vote; had never established an apolitical, professional class of election managers; and had no proper central electoral commission to set standards and lay down basic rules for everyone to follow, free of political interference.

In the absence of such a body, every jurisdiction was free to play fast and loose with the rules on everything from voter eligibility to whether or not to conduct recounts.

"All these different systems in different counties with no accountability ... it's like the poorest village in Africa," the chair of South Africa's Independent Electoral Commission, Brigalia Bam, later exclaimed on a follow-up tour of Florida on the eve of the 2004 presidential election.

Much of that dysfunction harks back to the country's shameful racial history. To circumvent constitutional amendments passed in the wake of the civil war, southern states approved a slew of discriminatory laws and introduced literacy tests and good character tests (also adopted in parts of the north) that made it next to impossible for black voters to cast their ballots. James Vardaman, the despotic governor of Mississippi, admitted in 1890 that his state's new constitution had "no other purpose than to eliminate the n*gger from politics."

Even after segregation and Jim Crow voting laws came to a formal end in the south, modern politicians remained susceptible to the temptations of racist dog-whistles as a way of mustering the support of white voters and justifying the restriction of minority voting rights. Many southern states, for example, have persisted with segregation-era laws banning felons and ex-felons

from voting—a restriction that disenfranchised an estimated 6 million voters in 2016, a vastly disproportionate number of them black men.

The Republicans have been especially prone to such corruptions because they are now the natural ruling party in the south, and they have resorted to a similar playbook to the segregation-era Democrats: stoking resentment of northern elites and harking back to the "lost cause" of the civil war. They have also become increasingly insecure about their ability to win national elections. Demographic shifts have eroded their overwhelmingly white base of support, and they have so far resisted repeated entreaties from party elders to broaden that support by moderating their policy positions.

In many states—notably North Carolina and Texas—they have exploited their majority in the state legislature to gerrymander congressional districts to their advantage. While both parties gerrymander, it has become surprisingly common for the Republican party to win fewer votes than the Democrats and still come out ahead in the House or Senate or both.

After the fight over the 2000 presidential race, the GOP's response was not to sigh with relief that George W Bush squeaked into the White House but rather to cry foul about African-American voters being allowed to stay in line beyond the official poll closing time in St Louis and to initiate a long, vicious publicity drive to insinuate that voter registration efforts in poor inner city neighborhoods were in fact corrupt enterprises to stuff voter rolls and ballot boxes on behalf of the Democrats.

Often, Republicans seemed to be evoking the era of New York's Boss Tweed, when voting numbers were routinely padded by repeat voters, out-of-towners, foreigners, and phantom voters who were in reality pets, fictional characters, or stone-cold dead. Such practices, however, were sharply curtailed after the introduction of the secret ballot in the late 19th century and ceased to be a factor of any significance after the last of the corrupt big city

machines was brought to heel and reformed in the 1970s and 1980s. Voter impersonation—of the type Trump has invoked—is not a significant factor, and study after study has shown that while individual voter fraud does occasionally occur, it is rarer than being struck by lightning.

The specter of voter fraud was often invoked in the segregation era as an excuse to crack down on the rights of blacks and poor whites, and so it has proved in this century.

In the wake of Barack Obama's election in 2008, there was an epidemic of racially coded appeals to the electorate's worst instincts, including insinuations that Obama was not born in the United States and that busloads of illegal immigrants had poured over the Mexican border to seal his victory at the ballot box.

Party strategists, meanwhile, understood that to halt the pro-Obama momentum they had to stop minority voters and students from voting in such large numbers.

Most insidious of these efforts has been the introduction of strict new voter ID laws in Republican-run states across the country, because they have proven easy to sell as a common-sense antifraud measure. They also happen to create difficulties for voters—the transient, the elderly, students, the poor, all less likely to have driver's licenses or other government ID—who are disproportionately black or brown and tend to favor the Democrats.

A government study has suggested that the introduction of stricter ID requirements could shave two to three percentage points off the Democratic party total.

One brake on this trend used to be the 1965 Voting Rights Act, passed at the height of the civil rights era, which gave the justice department veto power over any new election rule or law passed in parts of the country with a proven history of racial discrimination. But in 2013, this so-called preclearance provision of the act was scrapped when the Supreme Court decided in a hugely controversial 5-4 decision that racial discrimination was no longer pervasive enough in the south to justify it.

Immediately, southern states including North Carolina and Texas passed stunningly restrictive new voting laws that have since been denounced in federal court as openly discriminatory and in violation of Voting Rights Act provisions that are still in force.

While it may seem astonishing to see such tactics being deployed in the world's most powerful democracy, they cannot be attributed solely to the rise of Trump. In truth, the politics of electoral combat have been heating towards boiling point for a decade and a half—and are the product of a political system that has never, in more than two centuries, resolved basic questions of democratic accountability and is thus unique in the developed western world.

He has also championed an interstate system of crosschecking voter registrations nationwide that independent studies have shown to be riddled with errors and that critics say is in effect a monstrous mechanism to purge the voter rolls.

Trump owes his political rise to many of the same impulses that have guided this trend in Republican politics. He was himself an enthusiastic "birther" and kicked off his presidential campaign with open appeals to anti-immigrant hostility. Even before the election he was warning of the risk of massive voter fraud and tying it in his supporters' minds to the specter of out-of-control immigration policies.

All that helps explain the extraordinary alarm and anger that Kobach's work with the presidential advisory commission has triggered.

When Kobach asked states to provide a dizzying array of data on individuals—including names, addresses, party affilliations, criminal history and more—the Republican secretary of state in Mississippi told him to "go jump in the Gulf of Mexico." Shortly after, the National Association of Secretaries of State, which is majority Republican, put out a statement reaffirming its commitment to "increasing voter participation."

"This commission is a fraud. And President Trump has chosen a fraud to be in charge of it," a former secretary of state of Missouri, Jason Kander, said when it was established.

It explains, too, why the Senate minority leader Chuck Schumer—suddenly in the spotlight following last week's cross-party deal on lifting the budgetary debt ceiling—saw the racist violence in Charlottesville, and Trump's failure to offer a full-throated condemnation, as a reason to shut down the election commission.

In a piece published in late August, Schumer condemned the "methodical and pernicious way in which [Trump's] administration is promoting discrimination, both subtle and not so subtle, in its policies and actions—especially when it comes to undermining the universal right of every American to vote."

"The president's 'Election Integrity Commission' and the actions of the attorney general are wolves in sheep's clothing. They are a ruse. Their only intention is to disenfranchise voters."

11

Corruption Is Even Worse Since the 2016 Election

Transparency International

Transparency International is a global civil society organization leading the fight against corruption. It has chapters in more than 100 countries and works to give voice to victims and witnesses of corruption.

A survey conducted by Transparency International in October and November of 2017 found that a majority of Americans felt that corruption in the United States had become worse in the year since the election of Donald Trump and that government efforts to fight corruption had become weaker. Suggestions on what to do in response to these findings are also offered, including providing greater protections to whistleblowers, ending shell companies, and offering greater oversight. The authors also encourage average citizens to use their votes to fight corrupt politicians.

The US faces a wide range of domestic challenges related to the abuse of entrusted power for private gain, which is Transparency International's definition of corruption.

Key issues include the influence of wealthy individuals over government; "pay to play" politics and the revolving doors between elected government office, for-profit companies, and professional

"Corruption in the USA: The difference a year makes," Transparency International, December 12, 2017. https://www.transparency.org/news/feature/corruption_in_the_usa_the_difference_a_year_makes. Licensed under CC BY-ND 4.0.

associations; and the abuse of the US financial system by corrupt foreign kleptocrats and local elites.

The current US president was elected on a promise of cleaning up American politics and making government work better for those who feel their interests have been neglected by political elites.

Yet, rather than feeling better about progress in the fight against corruption over the past year, a clear majority of people in America now say that things have become worse. Nearly six in ten people now say that the level of corruption has risen in the past twelve months, up from around a third who said the same in January 2016.

A new survey by Transparency International, the US Corruption Barometer 2017, was carried out in October and November 2017. It shows that the US government and some key institutions of power still have a long way to go to win back citizens' trust.

The results show:

- 44 per cent of Americans believe that corruption is pervasive in the White House, up from 36 per cent in 2016.
- Almost 7 out of 10 people believe the government is failing to fight corruption, up from half in 2016.
- Close to a third of African-Americans surveyed see the police as highly corrupt, compared to a fifth across the survey overall.
- 55 per cent gave fear of retaliation as the main reason not to report corruption, up from 31 per cent in 2016.
- 74 per cent said ordinary people can make a difference in the fight against corruption.

Office of the President Seen as Most Corrupt

The survey asked about the degree of corruption in nine influential groups. These included the national government (the president's office, members of congress, government officials), public officials who work at the service level (tax officials, the police, judges, local officials), and those who are not part of government but who often wield strong influence (business executives, religious leaders).

Of these categories, government institutions and officials in Washington are perceived to be the most corrupt in the country. The results show that 44 per cent of Americans now say that most or all of those in the Office of the President are corrupt, up from 36 per cent who said the same last year.

Additionally, many people hold an unfavourable view of big business. Almost a third of people in the United States think that most or all business executives are corrupt.

In comparison, judges are seen to be the cleanest, with just 16 per cent thinking that they are highly corrupt.

A higher proportion of African-Americans surveyed view the police as highly corrupt: 31 per cent, versus an average of 20 per cent across all those surveyed.

Weaker Government Efforts to Stop Corruption

The findings also reveal that people are now more critical of government efforts to fight corruption. From just over half in 2016, nearly seven in ten people in the United States now say that the government is doing a bad job at combatting corruption within its own institutions—this is despite widespread commitments to clean up government.

Voting Still the Most Effective Action People Can Take

At the same time, the survey reveals that despite increased concerns about the level of corruption, many people feel empowered to make a difference, demonstrating that citizens can engage with the issue.

When we asked what actions would be most effective at fighting corruption, using the ballot box came out top. Twenty-eight per cent said that voting for a clean candidate or a party committed to fighting corruption is the most effective thing they could do. However, this figure has declined from 34 per cent in 2016.

There has been a slight increase in the proportion of people saying that some form of direct action away from the ballot box would be most effective—speaking out on social media, joining a protest march, joining an anti-corruption organisation, signing a petition, talking to friends or relatives, or boycotting a business. Collectively, a quarter of people in the United States now think these are the most effective things they can do, up from 17 per cent in 2016.

A further 21 per cent said that reporting corruption was the most effective solution.

Fear of Retaliation Prevents More People from Reporting Corruption

In reality, however, many people don't come forward to report corruption when they see or experience it. When we asked why that might be, Americans now overwhelmingly say it is because they are afraid of suffering retaliation as a result. Over half of people (55 per cent) cited this as the main reason more people don't come forward: a substantial increase since 2016, when only 31 per cent said the same.

Recommendations

Americans have expressed their frustration with Washington and its elected officials in myriad ways. Yet there are things that can be done to ensure that institutions are clean and that taxpayer dollars are spent in alignment with the public's concerns and not just with special corporate and elite interests.

Transparency International calls on the US Government to address the following:

Transparency in Political Spending

Make all spending on politics genuinely transparent, with:

- real-time information accessible in online, machine-readable form to the public

- transparency on political spending by publicly traded companies
- transparency to the public on every level of influence, from political ad campaigns, to lobbying, to bundled campaign contributions.

Prevention of Revolving Doors
Stop the unchecked exchange of personnel among corporations, lobbyists and our elected and high-level government officials.

Establishing Who Owns What
End the use of anonymous shell companies, which can be a source of conflict of interest and/or vehicles for illicit activity.

Strengthening the Ethics of Infrastructure
Reinforce the independence and oversight capabilities of the Office of Government Ethics.

Protection of Whistleblowers
Improve and implement laws and regulations to protect the whistleblowers who expose corruption and other misconduct by the government and its contractors.

Providing Basic Access to Information
Increase access to information about the government, as a means to empower the public to fight corruption.

Earlier this year Transparency International highlighted how corruption and inequality can create fertile ground for populist leaders, but that such populist politics do little to actually stop corruption. The findings of the US Corruption Barometer 2017 reinforce this message. America needs actions—not just words—towards a cleaner and more open government.

Methodology
Transparency International commissioned Efficience3 to carry out the US Barometer 2017. Efficience3 directed a Computer-Assisted Telephone Interviewing of 1,005 respondents from October

2017 to November 2017. Respondents were selected using Random Digital Dialling. Data were weighted to be demographically representative of all adults in the United States aged 18+ by age, gender, social grade, region, rural/urban area, and ethnicity. Efficience3 conducted a comparable survey of 1,001 respondents for Transparency International from January 2016 to February 2016.

Due to rounding, percentages may not total 100%.

12

Incentivizing Corruption Fighters

Jermyn Brooks

Jermyn Brooks is Chair of Transparency International's Business Advisory Board and a member of the Steering Committee of Humboldt-Viadrina School of Governance's project on "Best Practices on Anti-Corruption Incentives and Sanctions for Business."

The author of this viewpoint suggests a combined approach of sanctions and incentives for fighting corruption. Genuine incentives such as preferred supplier status, assistance for capacity building, and favorable payment conditions might motivate those who previously had not shown much interest in countering corruption to help with the fight. The viewpoint suggests that positive reinforcement of those who help prevent corruption may work better than negative reinforcement, as punishment requires proof that corruption has already occurred.

A recurring theme at the 8th Gulf Cooperation Council Regulators' Summit in Dubai last month was the increasing expectation from regulatory bodies for effective sanctions, especially when targeting the financial services sector.

But little discussed was the motive for compliance. Why should banks and other companies get involved in supporting improved compliance and ethical behaviour? Increasing amounts are being

"Fear of punishment not enough to combat corruption. Give rewards too," by Jermyn Brooks, Thomson Reuters Foundation, March 5, 2014. Reprinted by permission.

written about WHAT companies should do, such as establishing an internal anti-corruption ethics and compliance program. But WHY companies should comply is far less elaborated. Are companies doing this only because they are required to by law? Are they doing this because it is the right thing to do? Or does it actually make good business sense?

In addition to a moral desire to do the right thing, there are typically two major motives why companies counter corruption: "fear factor" and "relief factor."

Corruption is illegal and companies responsible for it should be punished, often referred to as the "stick approach." Recent years have seen attempts to make corruption more costly through severe legal, commercial and reputational sanctions. But sanctions can only be applied if companies are actually caught engaging in such acts. And while we have seen a significant increase in law enforcement over the last years, there is still much that needs to be done. The latest Transparency International report on enforcement of the OECD's Anti-Bribery Convention shows that "in half of the [OECD] countries there is little or no enforcement against foreign bribery." Thus, in environments where sanctions exist only on paper, such threats are typically not a sufficient deterrent for companies. The fear of getting caught is simply too low.

No company is immune to corruption. Even companies with an outstanding program can be subject to incidents of wrongdoing. Nonetheless, companies with such a programme should be treated differently from those without. To that end reduced sanctions, so-called mitigation incentives, are increasingly offered under certain conditions for self-policing, self-reporting, cooperation or remedial actions. But again, sanctions can only be applied if a company is caught. And if sanctions are not applied in practice, no mitigation incentives by reducing the "penalty stick" can be given either.

So if doing the right thing is directly associated with a loss of business opportunities, and if sanctions are not (yet) applied

in practice, what else can be done to motivate companies more to follow ethical practices and to fight against corruption?

Carrot and Stick

An answer is a combined approach of sanctions and incentives. Especially in countries with weak law enforcement, offering a second type of incentives, so-called genuine incentives, can be far more effective than simply using sanctions alone—in other words a carrot and a stick approach. Such genuine incentives would show that preventing corruption makes business sense, and not only because the company can avoid sanctions or have them reduced.

There are already foundations for such an approach. For example, in the 2009 recommendations of the OECD Council for Further Combating Bribery of Foreign Public Officials in International Business Transactions, Article X.C.vi states that member countries should encourage "their government agencies to consider, where international business transactions are concerned, and as appropriate, internal controls, ethics, and compliance programmes or measures in their decisions to grant public advantages, including public subsidies, licences, public procurement contracts, contracts funded by official development assistance, and officially supported export credits." Genuine incentives within the business sector can include commercial and reputational advantages, such as (but not limited to) preferred supplier status, assistance for capacity building, favourable payment conditions, public recognition.

Providing tangible business advantages to companies that demonstrate ethical leadership can motivate even those which have not previously seen any value in countering corruption. But research from the Humboldt-Viadrina School of Governance shows that the value of this approach is often under-estimated or unknown to those seeking to advance the anti-corruption agenda.

Obviously, such genuine incentives are not a substitute for sanctions. But in addition to sanctions and mitigation incentives,

stakeholders should offer genuine incentives to business. If the commitment to counter corruption is linked to tangible business advantages, the likelihood is much greater that companies will actually make that commitment. Fighting corruption then becomes a business decision, supporting the moral desire to do the right thing.

13

Curbing Corruption with Transparency, Technology, and More

Augusto Lopez-Claros

Augusto Lopez-Claros is the Director of Global Indicators Group at the World Bank Group. He was Chief Economist and Director of the Global Competitiveness program at the World Economic Forum in Geneva and is also a former resident representative of the International Monetary Fund in Russia.

As an economist with the World Bank, the viewpoint author presents a number of strategies for fighting corruption around the globe. These include increasing the pay of civil servants to lessen the pull of temptation and increasing the transparency of the processes of government spending. Specific data like Transparency International's Corruption Index is referenced, as is the fact that New Zealand consistently scores high on the index. Chile is also commended for its use of the latest technologies in creating one of the world's most transparent public procurement systems.

Having looked at some of the ways in which corruption damages the social and institutional fabric of a country, we now turn to reform options open to governments to reduce corruption and mitigate its effects. Rose-Ackerman (1998) recommends a two-pronged strategy aimed at increasing the benefits of being honest

"Six Strategies to Fight Corruption," by Augusto Lopez-Claros, The World Bank Group, May 14, 2014. http://blogs.worldbank.org/futuredevelopment/six-strategies-fight-corruption. Licensed under CC BY 3.0 IGO.

and the costs of being corrupt, a sensible combination of reward and punishment as the driving force of reforms. This is a vast subject. We discuss below six complementary approaches.

Paying Civil Servants Well

Whether civil servants are appropriately compensated or grossly underpaid will clearly affect motivation and incentives. If public sector wages are too low, employees may find themselves under pressure to supplement their incomes in "unofficial" ways. Van Rijckeghem and Weder (2001) did some empirical work showing that in a sample of less developed countries, there is an inverse relationship between the level of public sector wages and the incidence of corruption.

Creating Transparency and Openness in Government Spending

Subsidies, tax exemptions, public procurement of goods and services, soft credits, extra-budgetary funds under the control of politicians—all are elements of the various ways in which governments manage public resources. Governments collect taxes, tap the capital markets to raise money, receive foreign aid and develop mechanisms to allocate these resources to satisfy a multiplicity of needs. Some countries do this in ways that are relatively transparent and make efforts to ensure that resources will be used in the public interest. The more open and transparent the process, the less opportunity it will provide for malfeasance and abuse. Collier (2007) provides persuasive evidence on the negative impact of ineffective systems of budget control. Countries where citizens are able to scrutinize government activities and debate the merits of various public policies also makes a difference. In this respect, press freedoms and levels of literacy will, likewise, shape in important ways the context for reforms. Whether the country has an active civil society, with a culture of participation could be an important ingredient supporting various strategies aimed at reducing corruption.

New Zealand, which is consistently one of the top performers in Transparency International's *Corruption Perceptions Index*, is a pioneer in creating transparent budget processes, having approved in 1994 the Fiscal Responsibility Act, providing a legal framework for transparent management of public resources.

Cutting Red Tape

The high correlation between the incidence of corruption and the extent of bureaucratic red tape as captured, for instance, by the *Doing Business* indicators suggests the desirability of eliminating as many needless regulations while safeguarding the essential regulatory functions of the state. The sorts of regulations that are on the books of many countries—to open up a new business, to register property, to engage in international trade, and a plethora of other certifications and licenses—are sometimes not only extremely burdensome but governments have often not paused to examine whether the purpose for which they were introduced is at all relevant to the needs of the present. Rose-Ackerman (1998) suggests that "the most obvious approach is simply to eliminate laws and programs that breed corruption."

Replacing Regressive and Distorting Subsidies with Targeted Cash Transfers

Subsidies are another example of how government policy can distort incentives and create opportunities for corruption. According to an IMF study (2013), consumer subsidies for energy products amount to some $1.9 trillion per year, equivalent to about 2.5 percent of global GDP or 8 percent of government revenues. These subsidies are very regressively distributed, with over 60 percent of total benefits accruing to the richest 20 percent of households, in the case of gasoline. Removing them could result in a significant reduction in CO_2 emissions and generate other positive spillover effects. Subsidies often lead to smuggling, to shortages, and to the emergence of black markets. Putting aside the issue of the opportunity costs (how many schools could be built

with the cost of one year's energy subsidy?), and the environmental implications associated with artificially low prices, subsidies can often put the government at the center of corruption-generating schemes. Much better to replace expensive, regressive subsidies with targeted cash transfers.

Establishing International Conventions

Because in a globalized economy corruption increasingly has a cross-border dimension, the international legal framework for corruption control is a key element among the options open to governments. This framework has improved significantly over the past decade. In addition to the OECD's Anti-Bribery Convention, in 2005 the UN Convention Against Corruption (UNCAC) entered into force, and by late 2013 had been ratified by the vast majority of its 140 signatories. The UNCAC is a promising instrument because it creates a global framework involving developed and developing nations and covers a broad range of subjects, including domestic and foreign corruption, extortion, preventive measures, anti-money laundering provisions, conflict of interest laws, means to recover illicit funds deposited by officials in offshore banks, among others. Since the UN has no enforcement powers, the effectiveness of the Convention as a tool to deter corruption will very much depend on the establishment of adequate national monitoring mechanisms to assess government compliance.

Others (Heinemann and Heimann (2006)) have argued that a more workable approach in the fight against corruption may consist of more robust implementation of the anticorruption laws in the 40 states that have signed the OECD's AntiBribery Convention. Governments will need to be more pro-active in cracking down on OECD companies that continue to bribe foreign officials. In their efforts to protect the commercial interests of national companies, governments have at times been tempted to shield companies from the need to comply with anticorruption laws, in a misguided attempt not to undermine their position vis-à-vis competitors in other countries. Trade promotion should not

be seen to trump corruption control. Governments continue to be afflicted by double standards, criminalizing bribery at home but often looking the other way when bribery involves foreign officials in non-OECD countries.

Deploying Smart Technology

Just as government-induced distortions provide many opportunities for corruption, it is also the case that frequent, direct contact between government officials and citizens can open the way for illicit transactions. One way to address this problem is to use readily available technologies to encourage more of an arms-length relationship between officials and civil society; in this respect the Internet has been proved to be an effective tool to reduce corruption (Andersen *et al.*, 2011). In some countries the use of online platforms to facilitate the government's interactions with civil society and the business community has been particularly successful in the areas of tax collection, public procurement, and red tape. Perhaps one of the most fertile sources of corruption in the world is associated with the purchasing activities of the state. Purchases of goods and services by the state can be sizable, in most countries somewhere between 5-10 percent of GDP. Because the awarding of contracts can involve a measure of bureaucratic discretion, and because most countries have long histories of graft, kickbacks, and collusion in public procurement, more and more countries have opted for procedures that guarantee adequate levels of openness, competition, a level playing field for suppliers, fairly clear bidding procedures, and so on.

Chile is one country that has used the latest technologies to create one of the world's most transparent public procurement systems in the world. ChileCompra was launched in 2003 and is a public electronic system for purchasing and hiring, based on an Internet platform. It has earned a worldwide reputation for excellence, transparency and efficiency. It serves companies, public organizations as well as individual citizens, and is by far the largest business-to-business site in the country, involving 850 purchasing

organizations. In 2012 users completed 2.1 million purchases issuing invoices totaling US$9.1 billion. It has also been a catalyst for the use of the Internet throughout the country.

In many of the measures discussed above aimed at combating corruption, the underlying philosophy is one of eliminating the opportunity for corruption by changing incentives, by closing off loopholes and eliminating misconceived rules that encourage corrupt behavior. But an approach that focuses solely on changing the rules and the incentives, accompanied by appropriately harsh punishment for violation of the rules, is likely to be far more effective if it is also supported by efforts to buttress the moral and ethical foundation of human behavior. We will turn our attention to this in a future blog.

Social Media and Youth Activists in Anti-Corruption Campaigns

Mariana Ceratti

Mariana Ceratti was an online communications associate for the World Bank as of April 2012. She has written and edited stories for web and print publications throughout Brazil as well as other countries, including South Korea and Japan.

The author of this viewpoint—a young-adult activist in Brazil— cites videos from the 1992 protests in her country as well as the use of social media in the Arab Spring protests as the inspiration of her current anti-corruption activities. At the Global Youth Anti-Corruption Forum, Nicole Verillo helped highlight the important role of youth in the global fight against corruption, a movement that is increasingly creative, wired, and motivated, and which Ceratti details in this viewpoint.

Twenty-four-year-old Nicole Verillo from Ribeirão Bonito, São Paulo, was still a child when, in 1992, thousands of young Brazilians took to the streets, calling for the impeachment of then president Fernando Collor de Mello. "I watch videos from that era and ask myself how we could mobilize youth in the same way today," says Nicole, an anti-corruption activist since 2003.

"Global Use of Social Media to Fight Corruption Inspires Youth in Brazil," by Mariana Ceratti, The World Bank Group, November 9, 2012. http://www.worldbank.org/en/news/feature/2012/11/09/Brazil-youth-social-media-fight-corruption. Licensed under CC BY 3.0 IGO.

She brimmed with energy after listening to stories of youth who used Facebook and Twitter to incite the beginnings of the Arab Spring. "We can use pictures, videos and virtual leaflets to inform the public, organize protests and find volunteers, just like they did. Brazilians use Facebook a lot and social networks can help to mobilize people that wouldn't otherwise take interest in issues of corruption."

As one of 250 participants at the third Global Youth Anti-Corruption Forum this past week in Brasilia, Nicole had the opportunity to interact with some of the social media activists that prompted regime change in Egypt. The event highlighted the important role of youth in the global fight against corruption, a movement that is increasingly creative, wired and motivated.

Mobilization Network

In countries as diverse as the Philippines, Paraguay and Egypt, youth are using their digital skills to inform and inspire. They monitor the quality of public services with interactive tools, make official data available online and mobilize their peers through messages on Facebook and Twitter.

"Youth are very comfortable using social media to raise awareness, connect with the rest of the world and exchange ideas," comments Boris Weber, a Senior Governance Specialist at the World Bank.

The event also unveiled various initiatives that hope to inspire imitators in other parts of the world. In the Philippines, for example, an interactive website—checkmyschool.org—allows students to evaluate public schools across the country. In addition, the site permits users to contest official data via Facebook, Twitter and text messages.

"If you look at the demographics, you'll find that more and more young people are online," says 27-year-old Filipino anti-corruption activist Marlon Cornelio, from checkmyschool.org.

Taking Action

Around the world, the World Bank and the British Council support 15 anti-corruption youth projects with grants of US$3,000. One such project is Transparency Talks, which is based in Paraguay, a country ranked 154th in 2011 in Transparency International's Corruption Perception Index.

Through the project, a World Bank anti-corruption manual was adapted and distributed to students in three cities via CD-ROM. With the publication, launched in January, students can identify corruption cases and learn to take action. "We chose CD-ROM because there are still relatively few internet connections in Paraguayan schools," said 21-year-old activist David Riveros.

At his school, students denounced a corrupt principal, eventually winning his removal. "That was one of the most amazing results so far. Youth need honest leaders and good examples."

15

What Could Stop Corruption in America?

Represent.Us

Represent.Us is a not-for-profit organization that brings together people across the political spectrum to pass powerful anti-corruption laws to stop bribery, end secret money, and fix broken elections.

The organization Represent.Us supported the American Anti-Corruption Act in an effort to counteract various forms of corruption taking place in the United States. The viewpoint below details the key goals and points of the act, which include defining what constitutes political bribery, how secret money can be removed from politics, how the electoral system can be fixed, and how to enforce the rules. The American Anti-Corruption Act is a model act that was introduced in 2011 and is intended to help guide future legislation tackling political corruption.

Stop Political Bribery

Make It Illegal for Politicians to Take Money from Lobbyists

Politicians get extraordinary sums of money in the form of campaign donations from the special interests who lobby them. In return, politicians create laws favorable to these special interests— even when those laws hurt voters.

Under the American Anti-Corruption Act, people who get paid to lobby cannot donate to politicians.

"Fight Corruption in America: Stop Political Bribery, End Secret Money & Fix Our Broken Elections," Represent.Us. https://anticorruptionact.org/whats-in-the-act/. Licensed under CC BY 3.0 US.

Ban Lobbyist Bundling

Lobbyists regularly bundle together big contributions from their friends and colleagues and deliver them in one lump sum to politicians. This turns lobbyists into major fundraisers, giving politicians an incentive to keep them happy by working political favors.

The Act prohibits lobbyists from bundling contributions.

Close the Revolving Door

Lobbyists and special interests routinely offer public officials high-paying lobbying jobs. Politicians and their staff routinely move straight from government to these lucrative lobbying jobs, where they get paid to influence their former colleagues.

The Act stops elected representatives and senior staff from selling off their government power for high-paying lobbying jobs, prohibits them from negotiating jobs while in office, and bars them from paid lobbying activity for several years once they leave.

Prevent Politicians from Fundraising During Working Hours

Most federal politicians spend between 3 and 7 hours a day fundraising from big donors instead of working on issues that matter to voters.

Under the Act, politicians are prevented from raising money during the workday, when they should be serving their constituents.

End Secret Money

Immediately Disclose Political Money Online

Current disclosure laws are outdated and broken. Many donations are not disclosed for months, and some are never made available electronically, making it difficult for citizens and journalists to follow the money in our political system.

The Anti-Corruption Act ensures that all significant political fundraising and spending is immediately disclosed online and made easily accessible to the public.

Stop Donors from Hiding Behind Secret-Money Groups

Elections are being flooded with big money funneled through groups with secret donors. These secretive groups spend money directly to influence elections and make unlimited contributions to super PACs, which run ads to elect and defeat candidates.

Under the Act, any organization that spends meaningful funds on political advertisements is required to file a timely online report disclosing its major donors.

Fix Our Broken Elections

End Gerrymandering

Politicians are intentionally drawing the lines around voters in order to guarantee their own re-election and give their political party an unfair advantage.

The Anti-Corruption Act ends gerrymandering by creating independent, fully transparent redistricting commissions that follow strict guidelines to ensure accurate representation for all voters, regardless of political party.

Let All Voters Participate in Open Primaries

By controlling the primaries, the political establishment controls which candidates we can vote on.

The Act makes all candidates for the same office compete in a single, open primary controlled by voters, not the political establishment. This gives voters more control over our elections and more choices at the ballot.

Let Voters Rank Their Top Candidates, Avoid "Spoilers"

Outdated voting systems force voters to choose between the "lesser of two evils" at the ballot box or vote for a "spoiler" candidate.

Under the Act, voters can rank their top candidates, allowing them to support their top choice without fear of inadvertently helping elect the other party's candidate. If their top choice isn't going to win, their vote transfers to their second choice, and so

on. This makes it easier to elect independent-minded candidates who aren't beholden to establishment special interests.

Automatic Voter Registration

Our voter rolls and registration systems are outdated, error-prone, and costly. New and proven systems can save taxpayer money and ensure that all eligible voters are able to participate on Election Day.

The Act automatically registers all interested eligible voters when they interact with government agencies—whether it's when they go to the DMV, get a hunting license, apply for food assistance, or sign up for the national guard. Voters can always opt-out from being registered. Information is transmitted electronically and securely to a central source maintained by the state.

Vote at Home or at the Polls

Election Day is a mess. Forcing voters to take time off from work and their families to stand in long lines on a Tuesday is ineffective, insecure, and outdated.

The Act improves voter service by sending ballots to voters at home and allowing them to mail it back on their own timeframe or drop it off at a professionally-staffed voting center. Voters can still vote in person or receive assistance at a voting center.

Make Every Vote Count in Presidential Elections

The President's job is to represent all of America, but the outdated Electoral College means that presidential candidates win by spending almost all their time campaigning in roughly 8 "battleground" states. Everyone else's vote is taken for granted.

The Act encourages states to award their Electoral College votes to whoever wins the most votes across the country. This simple change would mean that presidential candidates would be rewarded for appealing to all voters, and the winner would be accountable to the entire country—not just the residents of a few battleground states. Everyone's vote would matter.

Change How Elections Are Funded

Running a political campaign is expensive, but few Americans can afford to donate to political campaigns. That makes politicians dependent upon—and therefore responsive to—a tiny fraction of special-interest donors.

The Act offers every voter a small credit they can use to make a political donation with no out-of-pocket expense. Candidates and political groups are only eligible to receive these credits if they agree to fundraise solely from small donors. The Act also empowers political action committees that only take donations from small donors, giving everyday people a stronger voice in our elections.

Enforce the Rules

Crack Down on the Super PACs

As a result of the Supreme Court's *Citizens United* ruling, the Supreme Court ruled that super PACs can spend unlimited money influencing elections, so long as they do not coordinate directly with candidate campaigns. Since then, there has been tremendous coordination between campaigns and their super PACs, making a mockery of the "independence" the Supreme Court said must exist.

The American Anti-Corruption Act enforces the Supreme Court's mandate by fixing the rules aimed at preventing and punishing super PAC coordination.

Eliminate Lobbyist Loopholes

The definition of "lobbyist" is weak and outdated. As a result, lobbyists regularly avoid disclosure, and former politicians and their staff can receive big money to influence politicians without formally registering as lobbyists.

The Act prevents lobbyists from skirting the rules by strengthening the definition of lobbying and penalizing lobbyists who fail to register.

Strengthen Anti-Corruption Enforcement

Agencies routinely fail to enforce the anti-corruption rules that already exist due to partisan deadlock—and when they are able to act, they often lack the enforcement tools necessary to uphold the law. The result is an elections system where even lax rules can be skirted or broken with impunity.

The Act strengthens enforcement of anti-corruption laws by overhauling the broken Federal Election Commission and giving prosecutors the tools they need to combat corruption.

Organizations to Contact

The editors have compiled the following list of organizations concerned with the issues debated in this book. The descriptions are derived from materials provided by the organizations. All have publications or information available for interested readers. The list was compiled on the date of publication of the present volume; the information provided here may change. Be aware that many organizations take several weeks or longer to respond to inquiries, so allow as much time as possible.

The American Transparency Project
200 S Frontage Rd
Burr Ridge, IL 60527
website: www.amtranproj.org

The American Transparency Project is a citizen-led investigation into challenges being faced by the ordinary American citizen. Facets of the project include: the documentation of troubling patterns of behavior on the part officials or multinational business entities, the reporting of attempted manipulation of Americans or their government and elected officials, and the hailing of American whistleblowers who, on moral grounds, have exposed corruption of institutions or officials.

The Center for Responsive Politics (CRP)
1300 L St. NW, Suite 200
Washington, DC 20005
phone: (202) 857-0044
website: www.opensecrets.org

The Center for Responsive Politics (CRP) is a nonprofit, nonpartisan research group that tracks the effects of money and lobbying on elections and public policy. Its website allows users to

track federal campaign contributions by lobbying firms, individual lobbyists, industries, and federal agencies.

Citizens for Responsibility and Ethics in Washington (CREW)
455 Massachusetts Avenue NW,
Washington, DC 20001
phone: (202) 408-5565
email: info@citizensforethics.org
website: www.citizensforethics.org

Citizens for Responsibility and Ethics in Washington (CREW) is a nonprofit and nonpartisan US government ethics and accountability watchdog organization. CREW works to expose ethics violations and corruption by government officials and institutions. Its activities include investigating, reporting, and litigating government misconduct; requesting and forcing government information disclosure through FOIA; and filing Congressional ethics complaints against individuals, institutions, and agencies.

Common Cause
805 15th Street, NW, Suite 800
Washington, DC 20005
phone: (202) 833-1200
email: CauseNet@commoncause.org
website: www.commoncause.org

Common Cause is a nonpartisan grassroots organization dedicated to upholding the core values of American democracy, including working to create open, honest, and accountable government that serves the public interest; promoting equal rights, opportunity, and representation for all; and empowering all people to make their voices heard in the political process. In this spirit, Common Cause serves as an independent voice for change and a watchdog against corruption and abuse of power.

Judicial Watch, Inc.
425 Third Street SW
Suite 800
Washington, DC 20024
phone: 1 (888) 593-8442
email: info@judicialwatch.org
website: www.judicialwatch.org

Judicial Watch, Inc. is a conservative educational foundation. It promotes transparency, accountability, and integrity in government, politics, and the law. Judicial Watch advocates high standards of ethics and morality in the nation's public life and seeks to ensure that political and judicial officials do not abuse the powers entrusted to them by the American people. Judicial Watch fulfills its educational mission through litigation, investigations, and public outreach.

News Media Watchdog (NMWD)
email: newsmediawatchdog@gmail.com
website: www.newsmediawatchdog.com

News Media Watchdog (NMWD) is an independent news website dedicated to keeping track of the latest current events and popular headlines. On the "Headlines" page a widget pulls RSS feeds from various sites to a centralized location. These feeds include outlets such as *CNN*, *Fox*, *MSNBC*, *Breitbart*, the *Washington Post*, *RT*, and more. The page is arranged in two columns, with left-leaning/liberal news located on the left side and right-leaning/conservative news located on the right.

Project On Government Oversight (POGO)
1100 G Street, NW Suite 500
Washington, DC 20005
phone: (202) 347-1122
email: info@pogo.org
website: www.pogo.org

Founded in 1981, the Project On Government Oversight (POGO) is a nonpartisan independent watchdog that champions good government reforms. POGO's investigations into corruption, misconduct, and conflicts of interest achieve a more effective, accountable, open, and ethical federal government. In 1990, after many successes reforming military spending such as a Pentagon spending freeze at the height of the Cold War, POGO decided to expand its mandate and investigate waste, fraud, and abuse throughout the federal government. Throughout its history, POGO's work has been applauded by members of Congress from both sides of the aisle, federal workers and whistleblowers, other nonprofits, and the media.

Represent.Us
PO Box 60008
Florence, MA 01062
phone: (855) 585-8100
email: info@represent.us
website: https://represent.us

Represent.Us was formed a year after the Anti-Corruption Act was drafted. Members work with leaders across the political spectrum to build power in their communities. They helped pass the first citywide anti-corruption act in Tallahassee, Florida, in 2014, and the first statewide act in South Dakota in 2016. Through Represent. Us, voters have passed more than seventy-five anti-corruption acts and resolutions across America.

Transparency International (TI)
Alt-Moabit 96
10559 Berlin Germany
phone: +49 30 3438 200
email: ti@transparency.org
website: www.transparency.org

From villages in rural India to the corridors of power in Brussels, Transparency International (TI) gives voice to the victims and

witnesses of corruption. TI works with governments, businesses, and citizens to stop the abuse of power, bribery, and secret deals. Through chapters in more than 100 countries and an international secretariat in Berlin, the organization strives for a world free of corruption. They are leading the fight against corruption.

Bibliography

Books

Sarah Chayes. *Thieves of State: Why Corruption Threatens Global Security*. New York, NY: W. W. Norton & Company, 2016.

Elizabeth Drew. *The Corruption of American Politics: What Went Wrong and Why*. New York, NY: Kensington Pub Corp, 1999.

Ray Fisman and Miriam A. Golden. *Corruption: What Everyone Needs to Know*. New York, NY: Oxford University Press, 2017.

Luke Harding. *Collusion: Secret Meetings, Dirty Money, and How Russia Helped Donald Trump Win*. New York, NY: Vintage, 2017.

Arnold Heidenheimer. *Political Corruption, Concepts and Contexts*, New Brunswick, NJ: Transaction Publishers, 2009.

Leslie Holmes. *Corruption: A Very Short Introduction*. New York, NY: Oxford University Press, 2015.

Susan Rose-Ackerman and Bonnie J. Palifka. *Corruption and Government: Causes, Consequences, and Reform*. Cambridge, UK: Cambridge University Press, 2016.

Robert I. Rotburg. *The Corruption Cure: How Citizens and Leaders Can Combat Graft*. Princeton, NJ: Princeton University Press, 2017.

Peter Schweizer. *Secret Empires: How the American Political Class Hides Corruption and Enriches Family and Friends*. New York, NY: HarperCollins, 2018.

Zephyr Teachout. *Corruption in America: From Benjamin Franklin's Snuff Box to Citizens United*. Cambridge, MA: Harvard University Press, 2016.

James A. Thurber and Candice J. Nelson. *Campaigns and Elections American Style*. Boulder, CO: Westview Press, 2014.

Periodicals and Internet Sources

Lee Drutman, "What we get wrong about lobbying and corruption," *Washington Post*, April 16, 2015, https://www.washingtonpost.com/news/monkey-cage/wp/2015/04/16/what-we-get-wrong-about-lobbying-and-corruption/?utm_term=.8789f599395c.

Breanne Gilpatrick, "Removing Corporate Campaign Finance Restrictions in Citizens United V. Federal Election Commission," *Harvard Journal of Law & Public Policy*, Vol. 34, No. 1, Winter 2011.

Newt Gingrich, "The Corruption of American Freedom," *Washington Times*, August 25, 2015, https://www.washingtontimes.com/ news/2015/aug/25/newt-gingrich-corruption-american-freedom/.

Max de Haldevang and Heather Timmons, "One of the US's greatest gifts to the global economy is under threat from Trump," Quartz Media, LLC, March 13, 2017, https://qz.com/927217/one-of-the-worlds-best-weapons-against-bribery-and-corruption-is-under-threat-from-trump/.

Michael Hiltzik, "Five Years after Citizens United Ruling, big money reigns," *Los Angeles Times*, January 24, 2015, www.latimes.com/ business/hiltzik/la-fi-hiltzik-20150125-column.html.

Glenn Hubbard and Tim Kane, "In Defense of Citizens United: Why Campaign Finance Reform Threatens American Democracy," *Foreign Affairs*, Vol. 92, No. 4, July/August 2013.

Karina Izquierdo, "How corruption is destroying the environment," *Words in the Bucket*, March 3, 2017, https://www .wordsinthebucket.com/how-corruption-is-destroying-the-environment

Michael Maiello, "Corruption, American Style," *Forbes*, January 22, 2009, https://www.forbes.com/2009/01/22/corruption-lobbying-bribes-biz-corruption09-cx_mm_0122maiello .html#1d7ac294224e.

Donald Scarinci, "Political Patronage is a fact of life at every level of Government," *Observer*, January 25, 2017, http://observer .com/2017/01/political-patronage-is-a-fact-of-life-at-every-level-of-government/.

Laurence H. Tribe, "Dividing Citizens United: The Case V. the Controversy," *Constitutional Commentary*, Vol. 30, No. 2, Summer 2015.

George Will, "The Corrupting Campaign Against Political 'Corruption,'" *Chicago Tribune*, July 2, 2016, www.chicagotribune .com/news/opinion/commentary/ct-supreme-court-political-corruption-mcdonnell-perspec-0704-20160702-story.html.

Index

E

embezzlement, 10, 15
executive branch, 27, 29,
    33–35, 45–47
exploitation, 15, 88

F

Facebook, 109
Fall, Albert B., 11
federal convictions, 42, 43
Federal Election Commission,
    FEC, 74, 79, 81, 82, 116
Foreign Corrupt Practices Act,
    FCPA, 19
free speech, 82–84

G

Geithner, Timothy, 10
gerrymandering, 88, 113
gifts, 41, 44, 51–53
Global Corruption Barometer,
    16, 17
Grant, Ulysses S., 10
Gumbel, Andrew, 85–91
Gupta, Vanita, 86

H

Henry, Patrick, 29
home ownership, 58
Humboldt-Viadrina School of
    Governance, 98, 100

I

income distribution, 54, 63, 68

inflation, 65, 70
Internal Revenue Service,
    63–64
Investigative Reporters and
    Editors, 41, 44

J

Johnston, Michael, 41–50
judicial branch, 22, 29, 45–48
Justice Department, 41, 42,
    86, 89

K

Kobach, Kris, 85, 86, 90

L

law enforcement records, 15
legal corruption, 41, 44–49
legislative branch, 29, 45–48
lifetime equality, 70
lobbying, 11, 15, 61, 84, 96,
    111, 112, 115
Lopez-Claros, Augusto,
    102–107

M

Madison, James, 9, 26, 33–35
Madoff, Ray, 58
machine politics, 15, 39
Maloney, Thomas J., 11
misinformation, 59
Morreim, E. Haavi, 52

V

venal corruption, 27, 28, 32
Voice of America, 37–40

W

Wallis, John Joseph, 25–36
Watergate, 11
wealth distribution, 54–56, 59,
    60, 62, 63, 72
World Bank, 16, 18, 102, 108,
    109, 110
World Institute for
    Development Economics
    Research, 60

Other Books in the At Issue Series

At Issue

| Political Corruption